After the Hunt
with Lovett Williams

Lovett E. Williams Jr.

Dedication

I dedicate this book, my seventh about wild turkeys, to my two daughters Mary Brooke and Heather Keane, who grew up with human-imprinted wild turkeys and endured a low place in the pecking order to which Heather's small spur scar attests. Living with wild turkeys is hazardous and I am sure Mary Brooke and Heather sometimes wondered which side I would take in the event of all out war with the turkeys. But war never came and the turkeys are now long gone. My girls are grown and I love them even more than I did the turkeys.

Published by

 **krause publications**

700 E. State Street • Iola, WI 54990-0001
Telephone: 715/445-2214

Please call or write for our free catalog of outdoor publications.
Our toll-free number to place an order or obtain a free catalog is 800-258-0929
or please use our regular business telephone 715-445-2214 for editorial
comment and further information.

Library of Congress Catalog Number: 95-82421
ISBN: 0-87341-421-7
Printed in the United States of America

Contents

Preface

One cannot say enough about the turkey. As a domestic animal, it is the New World's most important contribution to animal husbandry. As a game bird, it is the world's most highly regarded.

Those who hunt turkeys deserve high praise as well. I have hunted since age six and have always been impressed with the dedication and sporting attitudes of turkey hunters. They appreciate the wild turkey as a species and want to know it from A to Z. I enjoy writing for such people.

Hunting the wary wild turkey is the exclusive domain of the initiated, but there is nothing arcane about the wild turkey's appeal. I used to think that the wonder of it should be kept secret and personal, and I sometimes still have mixed emotions about that. The wild turkey lives in places where I like to be. It is hunted by the most honorable means and the hunt is a true test of knowledge and skill—and the skills acquired are directly related to success afield. The wild turkey is small enough to easily carry out of the woods but large enough to feed a whole family. It is easy to prepare for eating and is delicious and nutritious. The wild turkey is exquisite in plumage, voice, and spirit, and is a joy to know and to hunt. It is too much to keep secret.

It is the immense respect and admiration we turkey hunters have for our quarry that brings on a chain of changing emotions when we hunt. First there is pleasant anticipation of the hunt. Then, as we hunt, there is growing anxiety to make a kill, which, once contact with a turkey is made, evolves into dizzying excitement of the approaching opportunity. Finally, comes the thrill of taking the bird and the satisfaction of the achievement—topped off by the equally important announcement of success back home. Soon afterward, gradually and inevitably, there is a feeling that creeps in: Is the fun over already?

Then what? You have a dead animal on your hands. I know the feeling so well.

I wrote this book about how to avoid the letdown. When you hunt and kill a turkey, the game brought in is also a trophy that can be kept forever if you do the right things with the remains. Some part of every turkey hunt is worth saving. The only question is: What shall I save of this one?

My first turkey will always be my best—an immature hen, shot out of a tree, in the fall, after sunset. If I think of her as my best, it is obvious that trophy ranking is not competitive for me. Not for the first one, anyway.

However, after the first turkey or two, we begin to rate trophies by certain standards. If you think a gobbler is a better trophy than a jake, or that a twelve-inch beard has more value than an eight-inch one, you are conforming to a scale of trophy grading. Chapter 1 discusses trophy features, how they develop on the bird, and what rating standards are used.

An important element of trophy value is uniqueness. What could be more unique than a turkey with two spurs on one leg or a plume on top of its head? There are more thirteen-inch beards and two-inch spurs than there are gobblers with two snoods. If you are fortunate enough to take a specimen with unusual physical features, you have a real trophy. I will go into that in some detail in Chapter 2.

The grand slam is a hot topic for good reasons. When you take five different wild turkeys, you have five adventures to remember and five trophies to remind you. I have devoted a chapter to the grand slam in which I explain where to find these subspecies, how to identify them, and what important things differentiate their hunting.

I am an amateur taxidermist and have preserved many wings, tails, legs, bones, and whole wild turkey skins. I'll tell you how to prepare your whole trophy for a taxidermist and then get it to him or her, even from Mexico, where many hunters have met with disappointment because of difficulties at the border. I will also explain how to save the small parts that make good trophies. Those in quest will always be looking for a "feather for the cap" and, thankfully, the wild turkey has 5,350. That's all covered in chapters 4 and 5.

The turkey's voice is one of its most interesting features. With over twenty-eight calls, it is the most vocal bird known, and calling it is your most effective hunting strategy. The wingbone turkey yelper is unexcelled as a wild turkey calling instrument— and it has mystique. I have made a study of the wingbone in the last few years and in Chapter 6 I take pleasure in sharing with you what I have learned about making and using the wingbone.

As hunters mature, they tend to enjoy things they gave little notice to when younger and turn more to conservation activities, helping others hunt, teaching young people, and simply enjoying the atmosphere of the woods and hunting camp. In time, the pictures of your hunts will prove the most durable and important things you have, and if you take up photography of live turkeys, you will find more trophies out there than you could ever have taken with your gun. Chapter 7 discusses photography and voice recording.

Don't forget to eat your trophy. Most people know how to cook a domestic turkey, but a wild one deserves special care. Honor your trophy by eating it right. Chapter 8 covers that, in case you don't already know.

Parts of this book will not be particularly entertaining as plain reading material, but will be invaluable when you need the information. I suggest that you scan the book so you will know what's in it, read the parts that interest you now, and save the rest for times when it is needed. Don't lend it to anybody because then you won't have it when you need it.

Collecting and displaying trophies is a trait that arises from the same place in us as our spirituality and is as instinctive for humans as hunting itself. I am not a trophy hunter *per se* but I have found that a few mementos of the hunt create the right atmosphere to live in. When we hunt, we derive something of value that enriches our lives. Enrichment depends upon remembering. Who would we be if we couldn't remember anything? Trophies help us remember.

For the past one hundred years, almost every book written about the wild turkey has begun by telling how Benjamin Franklin promoted the wild turkey, in lieu of the bald eagle, as our national bird when the issue was being debated in Congress. I guess I have to say something about that, but I won't go into it very deeply because Ben did nothing of the kind. The closest he came was to merely mention to his daughter Sarah in a letter, after the debate was over in Congress, that he would have preferred the turkey. Further, from my reading of Ben Franklin, I think he was speaking of the domestic turkey, not the wild one.

I admire Ben Franklin, but I admire the truth more. That's why I write about turkeys rather than one of the many things I don't know anything about. Not that I know everything about turkeys—I'm still learning and always will be. If you know something I don't, tell me about it.

This is my seventh book about turkeys and I can think of at least seven more to write. Get my first six to go with this one and stand by for *Turkey Book Number Eight*.

Acknowledgments

I owe much to many people for their contributions to my work and writings about the wild turkey. Many hunters and biologists throughout the U. S. have sent letters and photos of both rare and common specimens. I find in my files a photograph dated 1963—sent to me only one year after I began my career as a wildlife biologist.

I would not have been able to write this book or do much else with wild turkeys were it not for the early part of my career spent as a biologist with the Florida Game and Fresh Water Fish Commission. The top administrators, Bob Aldrich, O. E. Frye, Jr., James A. Powell, H. E. (Gene) Wallace, and Fred Stanberry were always supportive. The people at the Commission that I worked side by side with on turkeys were invaluable, especially David H. Austin, Robert W. Phillips, C. T. (Truby) Lee, Tommie E. Peoples, Neal F. Eichholz, Jerry Brown, and Larry Barwick. I have also had a lot of support from magazine editors and publishers Chuck Spearman, Gerry Blair, Gene Smith, and Jim Casada.

The names that follow are people who made contributions to this book by supplying or lending specimens, photos, reports, or other things I needed. I have lost track of some of the people who sent photographs over the years and I apologize for that. If you see an uncredited contribution you made, let me know— I'll try to correct that in the next printing.

In alphabetical order, the many hunters and friends who helped in countless ways are Dennis Andrews, David Austin, Wayne Bailey, Dennis Baker, Brit Barnard, Glen Barnett, Randy Benton, John Brashear, Ed Broadwater, Les Campbell, Randall Champ, Fitz Chandler, Steven Clark, Ed Coleman, Wayne Creed, Mark Crow, Jerry Davis, Russell Davis, Randy Deleggie, Don Doughty, Roy Dowless, Jr., Pat Drips, Ben Duncan, James Dunlap, Neal Eichholz, Tom Eilers, Todd Godsey, David Greer, Sam and Steve Hembree, Roger Holmes, Paul and Lisa Huddlestun, John Hundley, Gregg Ielfield, the late Leon Johenning, Tim & Brandy Jones, Tim Jolley, Larry Joye, Eustice Kelly, Mark Koehler, Joe Kurz, Milford Kyler, James Lambert, Billy Ledbetter, Mike Licata, Austin Lossett, George MacBride, Gregory Marco, Charlie Marlen, Dale and Tony Martoglio, Richard Mason, Mike McAnany, Bill McDuffie, Bo McEwan, Dusty Monis, Edmund Moody, John Morelli, James Pack, George

Parkhurst, S. J. Prescott, Don Prickett, Charles Purdy, Donald Puza, Reed Scghweickert, James Schneider, Gene and Sam Seney, Joe Slaton, Gene Smith, Glenn Smith, Devin Spaight, Dan Speake, Curtis Taylor, Bill Thomas, Jack Thomas, Spencer Tomb, Pat Tuttle, Jeff Walker, Matt Wardon, Parker Whedon, Billy Wilkinson, Michael Williams, Ronnie Williams, Robert Witte, and Tom Yacovella.

The work of artist Paul Tofte on the range maps and skilled editing of Deborah Faupel and Melissa Warden of Krause Publications are much appreciated.

1

What's a Trophy?

A turkey hunter should know more about the wild turkey's physical features than the average person on the street does. Do you know what a wild turkey's "wattles" look like? Chickens have them, and most people think turkeys do too—but they don't. Now you know more than the average person on the street. Read on and take time to examine closely the next turkey you kill—you may be surprised about what you have been overlooking or didn't know the name of. Scan this chapter now and refer back to it when you have a turkey specimen to look at.

External Anatomy

The main external features of the wild turkey are labeled in Figures 1.1 and 1.2. The finger-like **snood**, also called the "dewbill," is located on top of the turkey's bill where it meets the head. It is well developed in the gobbler but barely

Fig. 1.1. *External anatomy of the wild turkey: 1) snood, 2) dewlap, 3) caruncles, 4) beard, 5) upper tail coverts, 6) tail, 7) tarsometatarsus*

noticeable in the hen. The snood becomes longer and dangles limply over the gobbler's bill while he is strutting or fighting, and in hot weather.

The **dewlap** is the loose fold of skin under the throat, sometimes incorrectly called the "throat wattle." The dewlap turns red with blood when the turkey's body temperature is elevated. The main function of the dewlap is to cool the hot turkey, much like a radiator cools your car.

The smooth round bumps on the turkey's head, neck, and throat are **caruncles**. The largest are on the lower throat below the dewlap. Small caruncles continue along the throat and neck in horizontal ridges. Caruncles seem to enlarge somewhat in spring, but they do not inflate with air during strutting behavior. Small caruncles occur on hens and on juvenal males.

The ear openings on the sides of the head are covered with small feathers. The other features of the head are the bill, nasal openings, and the dark brown eyes.

The color of the head is a body language that telegraphs the mood of the gobbler. A blue-gray or dull pinkish color is neutral, whereas bright white on the top of the head signals antagonism or mating intentions. The hen's head is bluish-gray the year round, but the gobbler's head and neck change from pinkish during most of the year to red, white, and blue in the spring. The red color is caused by the release of blood to surface vessels. The very top of the gobbler's head turns white when blood is withdrawn from the skin's surface.

I'm not sure exactly what some of the color changes mean, but you can bet the turkeys do—Mother Nature does not fool around with such things for amusement only. I know that changing colors are associated with fighting moods. I have seen human-imprinted wild gobblers show heightened antagonism at the sight of clean white tennis shoes. They paid much less attention to dirty ones. Dark red colors also sometimes excite gobblers to fighting.

The turkey's **beard** is a bundle of stiff bristles arising from the skin where the neck and breast meet. We will discuss beards at some length later. The **upper tail coverts** are the large feathers of the lower back that overlap the base of the tail feathers. The **under tail coverts** lie under the base of the eighteen very large major **tail feathers**.

The **primary wing feathers** are the ten pointed, black and white flight feathers at the end of the wing (Fig. 1.2). The

Fig. 1.2. *Major feather groups of the wing: 1) primaries, 2) secondaries, 3) greater upper secondary coverts, or "speculum"*

nineteen **secondary wing feathers** are the broad feathers that form the trailing edge of the wing between the primaries and the body, becoming successively smaller from the mid-wing toward the body. The **greater upper secondary coverts**, which I will sometimes refer to as the **speculum**, form the large metallic zone on the side of a turkey's wing. The speculum is especially noticeable in adults.

The scaly lower leg has the technical name **tarsometatarsus**, called **"tarsus"** for short. *Tarsi* is the plural form in keeping with the rules of Latin. It was once thought that the red color of the turkey's lower legs *(tarsi)* is caused by blood seen through the clear scales; however, dissection reveals that the red color is actually caused by a layer of red tissue, like a piece of thin red paper, wrapped tightly around the bone and ligaments. The color does not fade appreciably when the leg is preserved and is not caused by blood. If you want to see that for yourself, use a knife to peel back a leg scale.

The legs of young turkeys are not as red as adults' for two reasons: 1) the red pigment layer in their legs is paler, and 2) the color is obscured by gray-brown pigmentation in the scales themselves. The dark pigment in the scales is called melanin and is there to give strength to the thin scales of young turkeys.

Leg scales grow from their base somewhat like human fingernails. As poults grow older, the scales become thicker and stronger and finally are thick enough that strengthening pigment is no longer needed or deposited. Without the pigment, the scales are transparent, like your fingernails, and the red underlying pigment shows through.

A few young turkeys have red legs as early as November; a few are still brown even in late winter, but there are no strong seasonal differences in leg color other than the normal reddening process of young turkeys during their first year.

Leg color in adult Florida and Eastern turkeys ranges from bright pink to deep red, and I suspect that is true also of the other subspecies. When wet, legs are deeper red than when dry, but I have not been able to pin the variation on anything else. There is no difference in the leg color of male and female wild turkeys, but adult Merriam's turkeys sometimes have dull brownish legs, rather than bright red, as will be discussed in Chapter 3.

Leg spurs are normal on male turkeys, as they are on some other species of fowl. Spurs range in color from black to almost white; some are two-tone red, silver, pink, or flesh-colored. More about spurs later.

The lower legs *(tarsi)* of adult male wild turkeys are five to seven inches long from the upper joint to the bend of the toes and about one-half to seven-eighths of an inch wide at the spur. There are definite regional differences. The legs of the Merriam's wild turkey are relatively short—averaging around five and one-half inches. Specimens of Gould's turkey from northern Mexico have long and robust legs, averaging over six and one-half inches—the largest feet of any of the subspecies. The legs of Florida turkeys are as long as the Gould's, but are slimmer. Rio Grande turkeys have slightly longer legs than those of Easterns, which average about six inches. Average lower leg length, from longest to shortest, then, is Gould's, Florida, Rio Grande, Eastern, and Merriam's.

The other physical features that differ significantly among the turkey subspecies will be discussed in detail later.

Molting

A mature feather is a dead structure, like a human hair or fingernail, and once grown in, it changes color only slightly due to wear and bleaching. Major changes in plumage color are caused by replacement of feathers, a process called molting. Molting involves two steps: 1) dropping an old feather, and 2) growing a new one in the same place.

At the time of hatching, the poult's body is covered with fluffy brown and yellowish feathers called down. Tiny flight feathers can be seen at the wing tips, but they have to grow for about ten days before the poult can fly.

The down plumage is followed by the brown camouflaged juvenal plumage (Fig. 1.3), and that by a darker "intermediate" plumage of late summer and early fall. By fall, the young turkey has changed plumage three times, has acquired most of its "first winter plumage," and resembles the adult in plumage. The juvenile stops molting when the first winter plumage has been acquired and will not molt again until spring.

Adult turkeys molt once each year during summer. It was once thought that turkeys had a partial "prenuptial" molt just before mating season, but further research proved that such a molt does not occur (Williams and McGuire, 1971).

Feathers are molted sequentially a few at a time. By the time the third or fourth large wing feather in a series is shed, the one

Fig. 1.3. *Summer poult in juvenal plumage*

first molted has grown large enough that flight is not impaired. A molting midsummer turkey retains its general feathered appearance and the ability to fly.

Jakes begin molting first and usually have shed one or more primary and secondary wing feathers and some of their speculum feathers by the beginning of the spring gobbling period (Fig. 1.4). Breeding males do not begin molting until after the mating season; hens do not begin until after they give up nesting for the season. By winter, every feather of the turkey's plumage has been replaced in the annual molt. The

Fig. 1.4. *Wing of jake in early spring. The missing feathers of the speculum indicate the beginning of the annual molt.*

turkey has approximately 5,350 feathers—the exact number depends on age, sex, and whether you count down and **filoplumes** as true feathers.

Pinfeathers are the beginnings of new feathers that occur in substantial numbers on young turkeys all summer and during summer and early fall molting periods on grown turkeys. Pinfeathers are not often seen in large numbers on turkeys taken in spring. The few you do see in spring are replacements for feathers lost through accident.

Trophy Features

The anatomical features most valued as trophies are the beard and spurs of the adult male. They are good trophies because they are durable; easily removed and preserved; vary in size with age and body size; are not easily altered; do not change size appreciably when preserved; and are visible externally.

Beard development and growth

A beard begins to develop on the lower neck of a normal male turkey when he is about five months old. A wart-like bump sprouts a few filaments and a tiny beard begins to grow from the skin under the breast feathers. The beard increases in size as individual bristles grow longer and as new bristles are added on the edges. I think a few new bristles are added throughout the life of the gobbler. In a study of beards of adult gobblers of all subspecies, the number of bristles ranged from fewer than 150 to over 600 (Schorger, 1957).

Bristles grow from the base and are alive only at the surface of the skin. The beard is the only plumage feature that is not shed every year. If the beard is forcibly pulled off, it will not regrow in the same spot (as a feather or hair would) but sometimes new bristles will be added around the edges of the scar.

By the time jakes are one year old, nearly all have beards long enough to protrude visibly through their breast feathers. Average beard length at that time is three to four inches. Exceptional late spring jake beards are five inches long.

Normal beards grow in length at the rate of four and one-half to five and one-half inches per year. Wear does not become appreciable until the beard's length reaches eight to nine inches at about two years of age. At that length, the beard begins to touch the ground as the bird stoops to feed (Fig. 1.6). A gobbler with a ten-inch beard often steps on the end of his own beard.

Fig. 1.6. *Adult gobbler's beard touching the ground as he feeds*

By three years, normal beards will have grown about fourteen inches, but will have been wearing off at the tip as rapidly as they were growing. The longest turkey beards, then, would be those that best resist wear (Table 1.1). The attributes that would facilitate a beard's resistance to rapid wear are beard thickness, heavy melanin deposits, long legs, rapid growth, and size of individual bristles.

Thick beards would have more bristles, increasing the likelihood of a single bristle surviving to greater length. Heavy melanin deposits would improve the resistance to breakage. Long-legged gobblers would grow long beards before they began dragging and stepping on them. Particularly fast-growing beards would have a growth rate that is faster than the rate at which they wear off. The diameter of individual beard bristles is a factor because thicker beard filaments are better able to resist wear and breakage than are thin bristles.

The turkey's environment is also a factor—in northern temperate climates and in mountains, adult males experience winter beard icing that causes premature breakage of the longer bristles.

Table 1.1. Factors contributing to longer beards

Factor	Affect on beard
Long legs	Beard longer without touching ground
Thick beard	Less likely for all filaments to break off
Thick bristles	Bristles stronger, resist breakage
Heavy melanin deposits	Bristles stronger, resist breakage
Fast growing	Beard grows faster than it is wearing off
Mild winter climate	No icing to cause the beard to break off

It has been estimated that about two percent of wild Eastern turkey hens have beards (McDowell, 1956). In Florida, the incidence of bearded hens is less than one percent (Williams and Austin, 1988). Approximately nine percent of domestic turkey hens have beards. These are estimates. The true proportions would depend in part on the age structure of the population examined—a population with a high proportion of old hens would have more hens with beards.

Most hen beards are six to eight inches long and are thin. The longest I know of was nine and one-half inches, taken by George MacBride in Pennsylvania. Nearly all have a crease across them about two inches from the base (Fig. 1.7), which may be caused by being folded under the breast as the hen sits on the nest during incubating behavior.

Fig. 1.7. Most hen beards are kinked at a light-colored zone, as is this narcotized hen's beard

The beard crease is usually deficient in melanin, which gives rise to the possibility that the crease is caused by a mineral deficiency that occurs during egg laying. The hen's physiological processes borrow minerals from her bones to make egg shells and later replace the minerals in the bones during summer and fall. If a hen's body robs minerals also from the growing part of the beard, which I believe it would, that could create a melanin deficient zone across the beard that could not be paid back later because bristles are dead structures.

Whether or not a hen or gobbler has a beard is determined by genetic rather than hormonal factors. Field research has shown that a hen that happens to have a beard is able to lay eggs and raise young in the normal manner.

We do not know with certainty the function of the turkey's beard, but I suspect it serves mainly as a visible indicator of adulthood in males. It is of no advantage for a hen to have a beard and probably has a small cost to her metabolism and social life, which is why most hens don't have beards.

Why do domestic turkey hens have beards at nearly nine times the rate of wild hens? It is because they get their food and other resources from humans, and therefore experience no physiological penalty and have virtually no social life for a beard to hinder.

Spur development and growth

Leg spurs are used in fighting and are normal in the males of other fowl species besides the turkey.

At the time of hatching, both male and female turkey poults have a differentiated scale on each

Fig. 1.8. Tarsal bones—from an adult gobbler with spur core fused to the bone and from a fall jake that had not yet developed a spur core

lower leg that will grow to become the leg spur in males, but will remain undeveloped in normal females. As the spur scale enlarges in the young male, a core of bone develops under it. After about one year, the bony cone becomes fused to an underlying sliver of leg bone called the styliform process (Fig. 1.8).

For the first year or two, the growth of the leg spur is due mainly to enlargement of the spur core. The growth rate of the spurs begins to slow as the male's skeleton reaches maturity and I believe growth of the spur after three years is due mainly to the lengthening of the spur cap and not to appreciable further growth of the underlying bone.

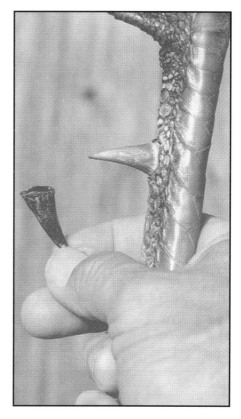

Fig. 1.9. The spur cap removed to expose the spur core

You can get a firsthand picture of the spur growth process by removing the spur cap from a recently killed gobbler's leg. Ring the base of the spur with a knife and pull the cap off (Fig. 1.9). Use pliers if necessary. You can glue the cap back if you wish.

Abrasion on the tip of the spur cap has an effect on the spur's ultimate length. Spur tips that contact rocks (Fig. 1.10) or hard clods of clay as the bird scratches will not be as long, or as sharp, as spurs of gobblers that scratch in softer mediums such as sandy, rockless soils. Turkeys that scratch in rocky and hard clay soils will not produce record book spurs regardless of their genetic makeup or age. They will also have blunt toenails.

A few hens have leg spurs (Fig. 1.11). The anomaly will be discussed in the next chapter. There seems to be no association between beards and spurs in hens—a spurred hen is no more likely to have a beard than is a normal one.

Fig. 1.10. *Foot of a 2-year-old Gould's turkey with blunt spur and nails (left); foot of 2-year-old Florida gobbler with sharp spur and nails. Note also the width of the Gould's leg.*

Fig. 1.11. *Leg spurs of a 3+-year-old gobbler and an adult hen*

Age Determination

Table 1.2. Anatomical features correlated with age

Feature	Level of usefulness for age determination	Comment
Beard length	Good	Up to 3 years[a]
Beard tip color	Good	Up to 3 years
Spur length	Very good	Up to 2 years
	Good	Up to 3 years
	Fair	3-4 years
	Poor	After 4 years[b]
Spur sharpness/curvature	Fair	Up to 3 years[c]
Leg color	Good	Up to 1 year
	Poor	After 1 year
Speculum shape	Good	Distinguishes juvenile
Tail margin shape	Good	Distinguishes juvenile
Shape of tenth primary	Good	In north
	Fair	In south
	Poor	In Florida
Length of lower leg	Poor	In adult
Head feathering	Poor	
Toe length	Poor	
Body weight	Poor	In adult

[a] See Table 1.3.

[b] Not reliable for exact year, but fairly reliable to classify in an age class "4+ years" if spur is over 1-1/2 inches long, and is sharp and curved.

[c] See Table 1.4.

Turkey poults can be aged with accuracy of about one week by measuring the length of their ingrowing wing feathers. However, after the last of the feathers of late summer are fully grown, plumage features permit us to classify turkeys only in what are called "age classes." The age classes are "zero to one year," "one to two years," and "three years and older." There is presently no known way to distinguish turkeys that are three years old from those that are older unless the individuals have been marked, as with leg bands, when they were young.

Fig. 1.12. Normal beards and body physiques: A) jake;

B) slim 2-year-old gobbler;

C) rotund 3+-year-old gobbler

Anatomical features that can be used to identify age classes are beard length and color, spur length and sharpness, leg color, configuration of the greater upper secondary wing coverts, shape of the tail margin, and sometimes, the shape and color of the last feather or two in the tip of the wing.

Features that are correlated with age, but not closely enough to be useful in determining age, include skeleton size, length of the lower leg, head feathering and color, toe length, and body weight.

Beard characteristics and age

Gobblers can be classified accurately into the three age classes by beard characteristics (Table 1.3, Fig. 1.5). Beyond the third year, it's anybody's guess.

The jake. "Jakes" are male turkeys up to and just beyond one year old. Features that confirm jakes are a short stubby beard, very small leg spurs (mere "buttons") and certain plumage features. Jakes will strut and gobble but do not normally mate.

When does a jake become an adult gobbler? During the spring and summer following the mating season, when the jake is in his second year of life, he replaces his first winter plumage with feathers that are identical to the plumage of older gobblers and, like other turkeys, he will replace that plumage each summer thereafter. His beard normally exceeds six inches (often over eight inches) by the end of his second summer; thus, for all practical purposes, a jake becomes an adult gobbler in summer and fall of his second year.

From the turkey hunter's perspective, it doesn't much matter where the line is drawn because the young turkey is a "jake" in the spring hunting season and will be an "adult" gobbler if you see him again in the fall.

The two-year-old gobbler. Two-year-old gobblers will attempt to participate in the mating process unless they are temporarily cast in a subdominant role. Even so, they are reproductively fertile and participate as bodyguards for a dominant gobbler. Identifying a two-year-old gobbler by beard characteristics requires an understanding of the wear characteristics of beards.

The black color of normal turkey beards is caused by a pigment called melanin that colors and strengthens feathers, leg scales, hair, skin, and beard bristles. Newly emerging bristles usually contain only a small amount of melanin, which

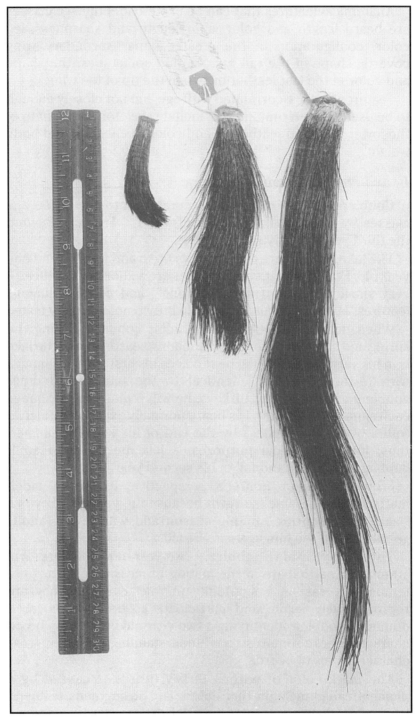

Fig. 1.5. Gobbler beards, left to right: jake, 1-year-old, 3+-year-old

makes new bristles somewhat amber or straw colored on their tips. Since the tips of all the beard bristles of a jake are new and low in melanin, his beard tip is normally slightly amber colored in transmitted light.

A two-year-old gobbler of normal beard growth will have a beard that has grown to nine or ten inches, and many of the bristles will still have their original amber tips because they will not have had time to wear off. So, the tip of a two-year-old's beard will be mostly amber colored in transmitted light. You may have to hold the beard at the correct angle to the light source to see that.

Under magnification, you can see that many of the bristles of a two-year-old gobbler are tapered and smooth rather than broken off, which further indicates that they are the original tips. So, a gobbler with a nine- to ten-inch beard with most of its bristles unbroken and amber-tipped, is only two years old.

The proverbial "six-inch beard" is not commonly obtained during open hunting seasons because that length is reached in midsummer during the gobbler's second year of life, before the opening of fall hunting season. A few short beards are taken in northern states where hatching is late and fall hunting is early, but even these will mostly be a little longer than six inches if you measure them carefully.

The three-year old gobbler. Distinguishing two-year-olds from three-plus-year-olds is a judgment call that I believe is about ninety percent accurate if everything is properly accounted for.

By the fall hunting season when a gobbler is two and one-half years old, the beard tip will have grown nearly three inches longer since last spring and will have only a small amount of amber color remaining in the tip because it will have worn off during the previous summer. Under magnification, you can see that the beard bristle tips are mostly broken. There will usually be a few amber bristle tips because a few new bristles are continually coming in, but the beard will have lost its two-year-old character. So, a fall gobbler that has a mainly black-tipped beard of at least ten inches is at least two and one-half years old.

When the same gobbler is three years old the following spring, his beard will look the same—the tip will be mostly black, the bristles will be mostly broken off, and only a few bristles will be amber colored. He cannot be distinguished

Fig. 1.13. Early summer adult gobbler with beard touching the ground. Part of his speculum has been molted in the annual molt.

from older gobblers by looking at his beard but he can be distinguished from a spring two-year-old. He is at least three years old.

The grayish look that some beards have is due to light reflected by microscopic scales on the bristle surfaces. The gray is more noticeable near the beard's base and on bristles inside the beard because the loose scales do not get rubbed away as easily there.

Some hunters say that Merriam's turkeys have shorter beards than do the other subspecies and some believe that Florida turkeys tend to have longer beards, on average, than any other subspecies. In one study of the turkey's beard, A. W.

Table 1.3. Beard characteristics useful in determining age of turkeys[a]

Beard length	Color of beard tip	Age of gobbler
Less than 4-1/2 inches	Amber	1 year or younger
4-1/2 to 8-1/2 inches	Amber	1-1/2 years (fall)
8-1/2 to 10-1/2 inches	Amber	2 years (spring)
10-1/2 inches or longer	Black	3 years or older

[a] From Williams (1989).

Schorger (1957) found no differences among the subspecies. However, Schorger did not know the exact age of the specimens in his sample and did not understand the beard development process or the factors affecting ultimate beard length. It was therefore not possible for him to adequately address the question of beard length differences among subspecies. There may be average differences in beard length among populations attributable to the factors listed in Table 1.1 and to genetic factors. In the north, beard icing alone could be a large factor. However, the longest beard presently on record, which exceeded seventeen inches (Langston, 1995, NWTF records), belonged to an Eastern wild turkey taken in Wisconsin.

Spurs as age indicators

Spurs are more useful than beards for estimating age beyond three years. The criteria I will discuss are based mainly on observations of known age Florida and Eastern specimens from the southern U.S.

The spur begins to grow before the poult hatches and it becomes a bluntly rounded spur about half an inch long in the typical 1-year-old jake, a bluntly pointed spur of 3/4- to 7/8-inches in 1-1/2 to 2-year-olds, and a pointed spur of slightly over 1 inch in most specimens that are 3 years of age (Fig. 1.14, Table 1.4).

I have measured spurs that were just under 2 inches long on known-age gobblers 5-1/2 to 7-1/2 years old. The spurs were very sharp and curved. Gobblers that old are rare. On the smaller end of the scale, I have examined a few spurs of known-age 3-year-olds that were only slightly over 1 inch long. They too were sharp and slightly up-curved. My observations suggest that a gobbler with a sharp, curved spur longer than 1-3/8 inches is at least 3 years old and one with a spur longer than that is probably older.

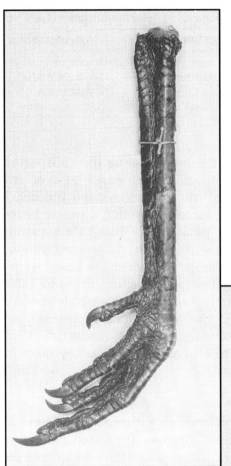

Fig. 1.14. Spurs of known-age gobblers: A) fall jake;

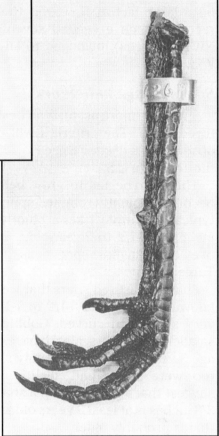

B) spring jake;

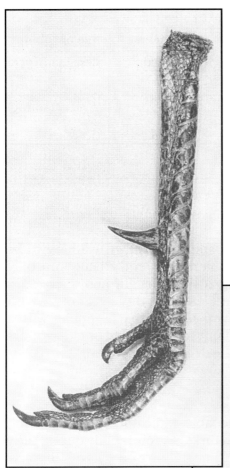

C) 2-year-old;

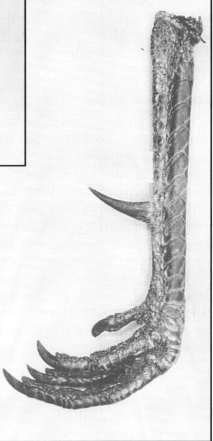

D) 3+-year-old

Table 1.4. Estimating gobbler age by spur characteristics[a]

Length (inches)	Curvature	Sharpness	Age of gobbler
Less than 1/2	—	Rounded	Less than 1 year
1/2 to 7/8	Straight	Blunt	1-1/2 years (fall) 2 years (spring)
1 to 1-1/2	Slight	Pointed	2-3 years
Over 1-1/2	Curved	Sharp	> 4+ years[b]

[a] Based on Williams (1989) with modifications.

[b] There is an increasing margin of error in this and older age estimates.

Until more is known about spur growth, we will have to be content with separating gobblers with confidence into only three age classes according to spur length and sharpness: jake, two-year-old, and at least a three-year-old. With somewhat less confidence, you can say that a gobbler with a sharp 1-1/2-inch spur is probably four years old or older. Spurs longer than two inches are extremely rare (Langston, 1995, NWTF records).

Body size and age

Weight alone is not a reliable indicator of age in adult turkeys. Like most birds, wild turkeys grow rapidly during early life and reach full size by the time they are of reproductive age. Increases in body weight after that are relatively small and due mostly to increased body fat.

Healthy grown turkeys have more body fat in spring than in other seasons. Body fat (and weight) falls during spring, is lowest in summer after the stresses of reproduction, and increases steadily during late summer and fall as the birds replace fat reserves, reaching maximum weight again in spring. Thus, a healthy adult gobbler's physique is sleek and lanky in fall and rotund and flabby-breasted in spring. A large deposit of fat on the breast, called the "breast sponge," produces the pot-bellied effect.

Turkeys in the northern and upper midwestern U. S. tend to be larger than turkeys in southern latitudes. An outstanding exception are the turkeys of the mountains of Mexico, which are the heaviest of all when they are fat. That will be discussed further in connection with grand slam hunting.

Regardless of the region, male turkeys are nearly twice as large as females of the same age, and maximum weights by age class and sex are nearly twice the minimum weights. Typical young-of-the-year hens weigh five to nine pounds, young fall gobblers nine to fifteen pounds, adult hens seven to twelve pounds, and adult fall gobblers weigh fourteen to twenty pounds. Although turkeys tend to be heavier as they grow older, they sometimes lose weight from one year to the next.

Pointed outer primaries of the young

The ten primary wing feathers of very young turkeys are more pointed, more brown, and have a fainter barring pattern than the same feathers of adults. During the poult's first summer, the pointed feathers in the wings are replaced with the adult type except at the very tip of the wing (Fig. 1.15). The retained pointed juvenal feather can be used to distinguish the young from adults.

Turkey populations in the northern U.S. stop molting after replacing the eighth primary, leaving two pointed feathers in the wing tip. Eastern wild turkey populations in the southern U.S. retain only one pointed primary (Fig. 1.15) and turkeys in south Florida often retain none.

Secondary wing covert configuration

Since many young turkeys in the southern U.S. replace all their primary wing feathers in the summer molt, it is not possible to distinguish them from adults by examining the wing feathers alone. The old books cannot be changed, so a misconception abounds that the wing tips are the best way to distinguish young of the year. There is a more reliable way.

Young turkeys rarely replace their juvenal secondary wing coverts prematurely in fall. For that reason, the configuration of the speculum (technically called "greater upper secondary wing coverts") is a more reliable way to determine age class (Williams, 1961). The speculum also permits field identification of live young and old hens without handling the specimens.

The irregular shape and dull-colored middle of the speculum of the typical juvenile (Fig. 1.15) is caused by the molting routine during the first summer of life. When the speculum is being acquired through the replacement of juvenal feathers, the turkey is small and the feathers are correspondingly small. As the bird becomes larger, each feather in the series tends to

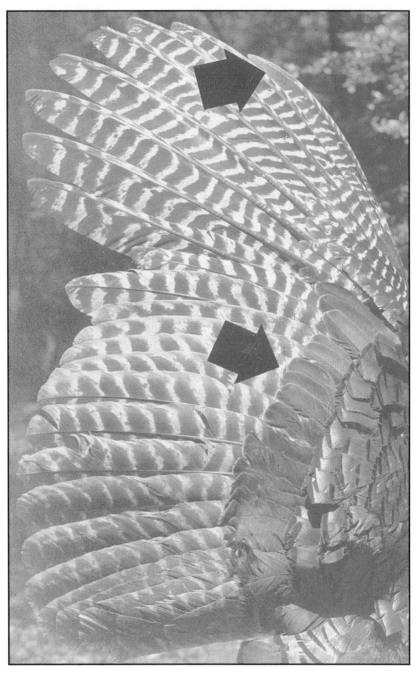

Fig. 1.15. *Wing of fall Eastern jake with single pointed primary feather and typical narrow speculum—normal plumage features of immature turkeys*

be larger to match the increasing size of the bird, and there is a parallel trend from dull brown colors in summer to shiny blackish colors in feathers acquired in fall. Compare the speculum of the adult in Figure 1.2 with that of the juvenile in Figure 1.15.

In the young gobbler, other physical features besides the speculum confirm age; for example, the stubby beard and small spurs. This is not so in the hen, which is why the configuration of the speculum is an important age indicator in females.

Extended middle tail feathers

The rapid increase in the body size of poults in summer produces a much heavier bird that needs a larger tail surface in order to fly well. A molting process similar to the speculum change occurs in the young turkey's tail. Rather than replacing the entire tail, only the small feathers of the middle tail are replaced. When these feathers are fully in, they create the well-known extended middle tail feathers of the juvenile (Fig. 1.16).

The extended portion consists of four to eight feathers, with six being the usual number. The extended effect occurs in both sexes, but is more prominent in young males than in young females. The longer central tail feathers of the young turkey persist until the annual molt in the turkey's second year of life.

In a few cases, young turkeys replace all their tail feathers in their first summer, rather than only the middle portion, and thereby have rounded tails similar to adults. That is unusual, however.

That's enough about turkey molting for most readers, but it is not the whole story. For a more detailed discussion of wild turkey plumages and molt, see my book *Studies of the Wild Turkey in Florida* (Williams and Austin, 1988).

Leg color changes with age

As mentioned earlier, juvenal turkeys have grayish-brown legs while adults have pink or red legs. This is not an important characteristic for aging males because of their other obvious age-related features such as the beard and spurs. However, the brownish leg color of the juvenile is sometimes useful in determining age class of dismembered female specimens in fall.

Fig. 1.16. Tails of young turkeys illustrating acquisition of the extended middle tail: A) juvenal middle tail feathers of a summer jake; B) the juvenal middle feathers have been dropped by early fall; new and larger middle feathers are growing in;

C) extended middle tail of fall jakes

Trophy Scoring

The late Dave Harbour (1983), described a trophy scoring system based on body weight, beard length, and spur length, that followed one that I helped develop for the Florida Chapter of the National Wild Turkey Federation. Harbour's system was later adopted by the national organization. I know of no other scoring system in current use for wild turkeys.

To register a specimen with the NWTF, you must be a Federation member. There is a small fee. Categories exist for hens and gobblers, and for Eastern, Florida, Rio Grande, Merriam's, and Gould's subspecies. There are categories for certain anomalous conditions such as multiple beards as well. The NWTF system also registers the Ocellated Turkey. The NWTF maintains a permanent record of overall scores as well as separate scores for beards, spurs, and body weight. The records are published from time to time. No prizes are given, but a certificate suitable for framing is awarded.

Here is a summary of the present NWTF scoring system. The beard is measured in inches to 1/16 from the middle of the base to the tip of the longest bristle (Fig. 1.17). Although the rules do not say so, beard bristles that are dislodged (not connected to the base) should not be measured and beards that are held together at the base by glue or other adhesive should be disqualified because they could easily have been altered.

Each spur is measured from the point where it arises on the leg, to its tip. The measurement is taken along the outside of the spur's arch, not straight across. A measurement straight across would be called the "chord" of the spur, which is not used in the NWTF system.

The curvature makes it necessary to use a flexible ruler, or you can place an index card against the leg at the base of the spur and bend the paper along the curve of the spur, marking the spot where the tip touches the card (Fig. 1.18). Then measure the spur length from the card.

Trophy score is determined by a formula designed to give more value to spur and beard length than to body weight. The formula is body weight (x 1)+ beard length (x 2)+ left spur (x 10)+ right spur (x 10)= score.

Weight is measured in pounds and is used directly. Beard length is measured in inches to 1/16 and multiplied by 2. The length of each spur is measured in inches to 1/16 and

Fig. 1.17. *Making a beard measurement from the base to the tip of the longest bristle*

multiplied by 10. All values are converted to the decimal system (Table 1.5) and added together for the total point score.

Using a hypothetical turkey weighing 18 pounds 4 ounces with a 10-12/16-inch beard, left spur 1 inch and right spur 1-2/16-inch, the decimal conversions of the measurements would be 18.25, 10.75, 1.0, and 1.125. The adjusted values, after multiplying weight value by 1, beard value by 2 and each spur value by 10, would be 18.25, 21.50, 10.0 and 11.25 for an overall score of 61.0.

The NWTF requires photographs and other documentation of outstanding specimens. If you are interested in turkey trophy scoring, contact the NWTF at P. O. Box 530, Edgefield, South Carolina 29824-0530 for the current rules and entry forms.

I have learned of turkeys being registered in the NWTF system that ranked high in total score because of their unusually heavy body weight. I have examined some of those birds myself and could tell from their physical features that they were derived partly from game farm strains.

Fig. 1.18. *Making a spur measurement along the longest curved edge*

Since game farm turkeys are partly from domestic strains, they are often heavier than turkeys of pure wild descent. Game farm turkeys are released throughout the country every year, mostly on a private basis. The people who sell them often claim they are pure wild and many of those who release the stock believe that. Hunters who shoot released turkeys are not capable of detecting evidence of game farm ancestry, and when they take such a bird they may register it in the NWTF system if it is very large. The NWTF system makes no provision for disqualifying game farm turkeys, thus the heavy birds will go into the record books and rank very high in overall score.

The system described by Dave Harbour took that possibility into account by multiplying beard length by a factor of two and spur length by a factor of ten, but it now appears that the provision does not adequately offset the weight factor of fat game farm strains.

Table 1.5. Converting ounces and inches to decimal equivalents

Ounces to decimal equivalent	Inches to decimal equivalent
1 oz. = .0625 lb.	1/8 in. = .1250 in.
2 oz. = .1250 lb.	2/8 in. = .2500 in.
3 oz. = .1875 lb.	3/8 in. = .3750 in.
4 oz. = .2500 lb.	4/8 in. = .5000 in.
5 oz. = .3125 lb.	5/8 in. = .6250 in.
6 oz. = .3750 lb.	6/8 in. = .7500 in.
7 oz. = .4375 lb.	7/8 in. = .8750 in.
8 oz. = .5000 lb.	8/8 in. = 1.0000 in.
9 oz. = .5625 lb.	
10 oz. = .6250 lb.	
11 oz. = .6875 lb.	
12 oz. = .7500 lb.	
13 oz. = .8125 lb.	
14 oz. = .8750 lb.	
15 oz. = .9375 lb.	
16 oz. = 1.0000 lb.	

There are other objections to using body weight in a trophy scoring system. Weight cannot be preserved for verification, as the spurs and beard can, and weighing scales vary significantly in accuracy—a set of broken or rigged scales, a gobbler stuffed with a little lead, a heavy hand, or simple conspiracy could determine the world record gobbler and nobody could ever detect the error, or deception, as the case may be. Furthermore, body weight of normal gobblers changes substantially during the year as they put on and take off fat. A specimen taken in early spring would normally weigh more than the same bird would if taken in fall. Should a gobbler rank higher because it was shot in April instead of November?

If body weight continues to be used in the overall trophy score, eventually all world record turkeys will be well fed game farm turkeys shot in the spring. In time that will subvert the trophy scoring concept. I don't know of any other game trophy systems that use body weight, except fish, and there is some doubt about the appropriateness of that. I think body weight should be eliminated from turkey trophy scoring.

Hunting Souvenirs Are Trophies Too

Sometimes you go for one thing and find another. I do that on interesting hunting trips and usually bring home something of value. I first realized how important the other things are as Fred Bear was giving me a tour of his museum when he first moved to Gainesville. He had game mounts in impressive numbers, types, and sizes, but some of the most interesting items to me, and to him, were the artifacts he had brought home from his many hunting trips.

On a recent hunt in Mexico I found a mountain lion skeleton in a dry creek bed and brought the skull and femur home. The skull was already bleached and now rests near some Indian arrowheads found on the same trip. From the lion femur bone I made the bell end of a wingbone turkey yelper. They both go well with the mounted tail of the Gould's turkey I took in the Sierra Madre Mountains, and are as much a part of the Mexico hunting story as the turkey.

2

Unusual Physical Features

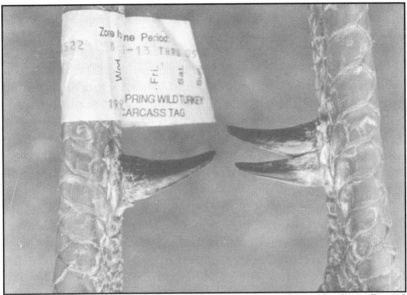

(Photo by Jerry Davis)

People who care little about twelve-inch beards or a big turkey that weighed twenty-four pounds will take a second look at a red and white speckled turkey or one with two snoods. A hunter fortunate enough to obtain an odd wild turkey specimen has a worthy addition for his or her trophy collection.

Many of the wild turkey's uncommon physical conditions occur too frequently to be considered aberrant. For example, the normal color of the underwing covert feathers is uniform gray, but a few of these feathers are sometimes barred. The dark inch-wide terminal band that circles the turkey's tail may be absent from the middle tail feathers and there are sometimes distinct metallic spots near the ends of the major tail feathers.

Upon close examination, no two turkeys look quite alike even if they are both within the bounds of normality. Variability is a natural endowment that allows the wild turkey as a species to deal with changing conditions by making use, when it is needed, of a trait that has lain rarely seen and temporarily useless in the population's genetic makeup. If being red should become advantageous to the survival of wild turkeys, you can bet your hunting boots that in a few thousand years or so red would be the normal color of wild turkeys everywhere.

Abnormalities are caused by genetic mutations, rare recessive genes, nutritional deficiencies, or injuries, and may involve the plumage, skeleton, spurs, beard, or other part of a turkey's anatomy.

Unusual Plumage Color

Plumage colors are labeled *albinism* (whiteness), *melanism* (blackness), *erythrism* (redness) and other technical-sounding isms. Colors in the wrong places can cause spots, stripes, blotches, and other abnormal color configurations. Most color freaks are caused by mutations or rare recessive genes and are usually "bilateral," meaning that if a body part or feather on one side is affected, the corresponding part on the other side of the turkey will be too.

The breeds of domestic turkey we know as White Holland, Broad Breasted Bronze, Bourbon Red, Narragansett, and Royal Palm, arose from genetic color mutants that occurred without warning and were selectively bred in captivity to emphasize the new colors so that they would breed true.

The most common off-color plumage type seen in the wild is the "smoke gray" form—a partial albino. The body plumage is nearly white, while the tail and wing feathers are only slightly paled (Fig. 2.1; and see color section). The lightest feathers of the breast are not immaculate, but when seen in the woods, a smoke gray turkey looks white. This mutant is responsible for many reports of "white" wild turkeys.

We have a mounted turkey hen in a dining room window where the morning sun strikes it at my Fisheating Creek Hunting Camp in Florida. After a couple of years I noticed the plumage was fading on the morning side. Now the faded side closely resembles a smoke gray turkey hen. Apparently, the plumage pigments most sensitive to sunlight are those that are missing in a smoke gray mutant.

The smoke gray color phase seen in the wild, however, is a genetic phenomenon and is not caused by bleaching. I examined two smoke gray poults that were only six weeks old. Even their underwing feathers, which had seldom been exposed to the sun, were pale. Their siblings and the brood hen were normal. I have a number of other reports of smoke gray hens with normal-colored poults.

Fig. 2.1. A smoke gray female turkey poult and her sister of normal color

Fig. 2.2. *Disrupted color pattern in a gobbler's wing*

In another color condition, the wing feathers and certain other parts of the plumage have a reddish, irregular marbled pattern (see color section). I have photographs of such a specimen trapped in West Virginia and another shot by a hunter in Florida. I have examined living and freshly killed specimens like it from Florida, Georgia, and Alabama.

There is a rare plumage in which the specimens have red bodies and partially white wings and tails with virtually no normal color or pattern (see color section). The major wing feathers and middle tail feathers are white, the speculum and back are red. I have photographs of gobblers like this from Wisconsin (Jerry Davis), Mississippi (Russell Davis), and Georgia (Mike Licata), and I have examined a mounted gobbler taken in Pennsylvania. I once saw a living specimen in Florida and I obtained feathers from such a specimen from a hunter. Wild examples look much like the domestic Bourbon Red breed. All reports of this mutant to date are of male turkeys.

Another mutant has pale plumage all over with the body feathers showing faded dark tips. It is somewhat similar to the smoke gray mutant but more closely resembles the domestic Blue Slate breed. I have heard of this occurring in the wild and have seen photographs of a hen specimen of game farm origin.

Sometimes a few wing or tail feathers are solid black, or white, lacking the normal barred pattern. John Brashear sent a photograph of a specimen with tail feathers and tail coverts that were very dark and lacked the normal vermiculated pattern.

Blotches of white in the wings (Fig. 2.3) are caused when a deficiency of certain amino acids occurs in the diet while the feathers are growing out. It is most often seen in young captive wild and game farm turkeys.

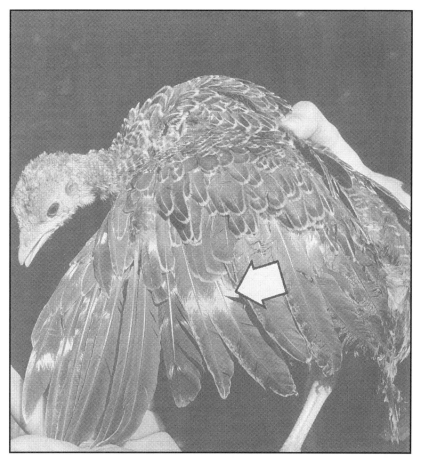

Fig. 2.3. *The white blotch in the wing of this captive wild turkey is caused by a common nutritional deficiency*

An adult gobbler from Levy County, Florida had white specks throughout the body plumage and abnormal white areas in the wings and tail (see color section). Most of the underwing coverts were white. It is the only such specimen I have seen or of which I have heard.

I have not examined a complete albino wild turkey, although the condition is known to have occurred in domestic strains and has been reported in wild turkeys. The White Holland domestic turkey breed was derived from albinos. A white specimen of Merriam's turkey, taken by James Schneider in Montana, had only one dark feather. George Parkhurst sent a photograph of a white hen he saw repeatedly in Missouri in 1991.

I have not seen a completely black wild turkey, although there is a standard black domestic strain. Such specimens would be called "melanistic." I examined a few nearly black feathers from a wild jake—its plumage had a suggestion of the normal color pattern overlain with a strong black wash. Alive in the woods, such a bird would look black. The feathers I saw were from one of two blackish jakes taken near Lake City, Florida in 1992. They had been seen together in a family flock and were believed to be brothers. Another black specimen from northeastern Florida was reported to me by Jerry Pionessa of Jacksonville.

Fig. 2.4. A single off-color alular wing feather lacking normal barred pattern

Fig. 2.5. Barred pattern in feathers under a gobbler's wing

The appearance of off-colored wild turkeys is no indication of ancestral crossing with domestic stock. In fact, I believe that little such crossing has ever occurred and that when it has, the resulting offspring rarely survived. The first generation following such a cross would be half wild and half domestic and would not survive in the wild even for the one year necessary for it to back cross with any native wild turkeys that may be present.

Fig. 2.6. *Loss of normal barring pattern in the secondary wing feathers, making the feathers much whiter than normal*

Consequently, miscegenation of wild turkeys with pure domestic "blood" could not have been widespread or serious. The massive releases of nearly wild turkey stock by state wildlife agencies is another matter. That could well have introduced domestic turkey genes into certain wild populations. That's a discussion for another time.

Fig. 2.7. Unusual color pattern in the central tail feathers of an Eastern gobbler

Killing off-colored specimens does not significantly reduce the local propensity. Such conditions are mostly caused by recessive genes or repeated mutations. Either way, the basis for the tendency is hidden in the population's genetics with only a very small fraction of the population exhibiting the trait. Anyway, off-colored turkeys are perfectly natural and you don't need to give nature a hand by shooting them in any kind of genetic cleansing effort.

Fig. 2.8. Frazzled tail feathers—cause unknown

Feather flaws

Feathers sometimes appear burned or partially melted. That, I think, is a result of injury to the feathers when they were in the pinfeather stage.

An unidentified agent, perhaps a fungus, sometimes causes deterioration of the main vane of tail feathers, making the feathers appear to have been stripped. The tail of a strutting gobbler with such a condition would resemble a sharptailed grouse. The condition probably occurs when the feathers are developing. I have seen a few feathers in this condition but have not seen it in life.

Sometimes the tail feathers are frazzled on the ends as though the tail had been shot off. I don't know how it happens. I once shot the tip of the tail off a turkey, but I never saw him again.

Some feathers show severe deterioration by late spring, which is why turkeys change plumage every year. White parts wear out sooner than darker parts because they lack the strengthening agent melanin. Wear is especially noticeable in the feathers of the back and shoulders. The white tips of the middle tail feathers of Gould's, Merriam's, and Rio Grande turkeys are noticeably worn by the end of the breeding season.

Feather lice lay their eggs on turkey feathers along the underside on the edge of the rachis. The elongated clusters of eggs create a white deposit that remains on the feather even after the eggs hatch. Underwing feathers are especially likely to have louse eggs in summer. Common turkey lice eat only loose skin and feather fragments; they do not bite the turkey and will not bite you.

Aberrant molting

Yearling turkeys normally retain a few juvenal feathers as part of their first winter plumage. Juvenal feathers are especially noticeable when they occur in the tail, wing tips, and speculum, as previously discussed.

Fig. 2.9. Tail of a jake in first winter plumage with abnormally short middle tail feathers (Photo Richard Mason)

Fig. 2.10. Adult gobbler with uneven tail margin

Sometimes a young turkey molts parts of its plumage sooner than normal. When one replaces its tail feathers in early fall, a rounded tail margin, similar to that of an adult, results. When one replaces its greater upper secondary coverts prematurely, an adult-type speculum results. Rarely, a young specimen molts its juvenal plumage entirely before the first winter and looks like an adult. Male specimens experiencing such a premature molt would be recognized as juveniles by their stubby beards and button spurs, but a young hen that molted completely wouldn't be distinguishable from an adult by her plumage. (You could still know her age class by her leg color, which would be brown rather than red, as discussed later.)

A jake taken by Richard Mason in Maine in 1990 had an indented tail (Fig. 2.9). A Florida gobbler had tail feathers of unequal length that made the tail margin uneven in outline (Fig. 2.10).

Also abnormal is a jake-like middle tail on an adult gobbler. One like that was taken in 1993 in Pennsylvania. Its beard was over eleven inches long.

A wild turkey normally has eighteen tail feathers—nine matched pairs on each side of the middle. Occasionally a turkey has ten pairs, and in rare instances will have an odd number, usually nineteen, with the middle feather unpaired. I have seen a specimen with twenty tail feathers but never one with an odd number, except when one had been pulled through accident. (In such cases, you can see the vacant slot where the feather was pulled or find a new pinfeather coming in.)

Freak Beards

Beards can be abnormal in at least four ways—multiple beards, beardless gobblers, beards shorter than normal due to flawed bristle structure, and odd-colored beards.

Multiple beards

I have taken three gobblers myself with double beards and one with three beards. I have examined specimens and seen photographs of many others. In the usual case, the largest beard is on the bottom and the beards are progressively smaller toward the head, giving the impression that the extra beards grew in later. There are a few exceptions to that, however. Multiple beards probably have a genetic basis.

Fig. 2.11. Gobbler with nine beards—the record to date (Photo Mark Koehler)

Multiple beards have been reported throughout the range of the wild turkey—several gobblers have been reported with up to seven or eight. Presently, a gobbler with nine beards, taken by Mark Koehler in Missouri, is the record (Fig. 2.11). Multiple beards are listed in Dave Harbour's book *Advanced Wild Turkey Hunting & World Records* (1983) but the book is out-of-date. The best source of current information is the National Wild Turkey Federation's records.

Beardless gobblers

Adult gobblers occasionally have no beard at all. Beards can be pulled off—I know of this happening to a human-imprinted wild gobbler living on my place in north Florida. A pulled-off beard will not regrow, but I once examined a wild beardless adult gobbler with new bristles emerging from the skin in front of and behind what appeared to be a scar where the beard had been forcibly removed.

I have examined at least four beardless gobblers (that I can recall) that showed no evidence of beard scars and probably never had beards.

Fig. 2.12. Beardless adult gobbler

Beard color and broken-off beards

The normal black color of a wild turkey beard is caused by a pigment called melanin. When melanin deposition stops for a period of time, as it sometimes does, probably due to illness, the portion of the beard growing at that time will be deficient in melanin and will be reddish or blond in color rather than black. When melanin deposition resumes, the part lacking black pigment will move outward on the growing beard and become a blond zone or narrow streak across the beard. Mark Koehler took the beard pictured in Figure 2.13 in Missouri and Britt Barnard took another much like it in Texas.

The blond streak is a weak zone, and the beard can easily break off at that point. When the entire beard breaks off, a jake-like beard is produced, similar to one reported by Paul Huddlestun (Fig. 2.14). That accounts for most of the adult gobblers seen with stubby, cut-off-looking beards. I have seen living specimens like that and examined a few in hand. Close examination revealed that the tips of the beard bristles were deficient in melanin where they broke. Roy Dowless reported two such occurrences in Florida specimens.

Fig. 2.13. Gobbler beard with blond zone across middle

Some hunters think incorrectly that stubby beards on adult gobblers are the result of the beard having been shot off by a hunter. You can test that yourself by shooting a beard sometime. You can't get a clean cut.

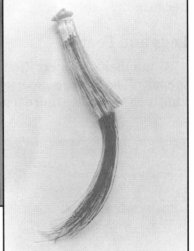

Fig. 2.14. *Jake-like beard on adult gobbler, caused by breakage of the beard at a weak zone similar to Figure 2.13 (Photo Paul Huddlestun)*

Fig. 2.15. Two-tone beard, part normal and part deficient in melanin

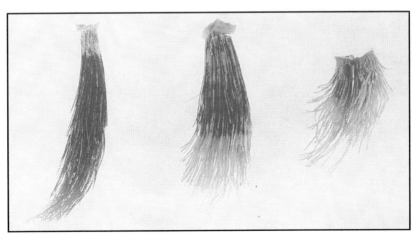

Fig. 2.16. One normal (left) and two off-color jake beards

Abnormal melanin deposition can cause very peculiar beard formations. One example is a beard with a blond base from which emerged a longer fragment of normal color (Fig. 2.15). In that case, the normal colored portion did not break off when the blond part surrounding it did. I don't know why only part of the beard would suffer a melanin deficiency.

A beard can be entirely white (or very blond) at its tip (Fig. 2.16). The white tip is caused by cessation and later resumption of melanin deposition during beard growth. If melanin deposition is not resumed, the beard will be completely white or blond.

Beards that are deficient of melanin are not very long because they abrade rapidly.

Legs and Feet

A number of aberrations involve the spurs, toes, and toenails. The feet are especially prone to injury. An animal with long toes that takes more ten thousand steps a day is bound to

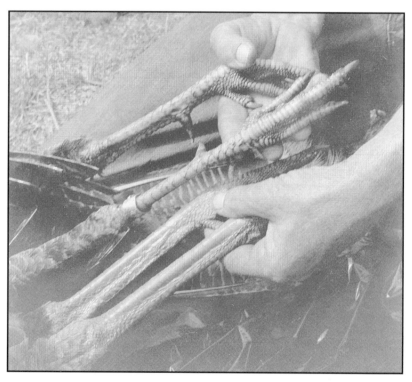

Fig. 2.17. Spurless gobbler legs (lower) and a pair of normal legs

Fig. 2.18. One large and one small spur on the same gobbler

step in the wrong place occasionally. Leghold steel traps account for quite a few stub-toed turkeys, but many abnormalities of the feet have other causes.

Spurs

Some adult gobblers have no spurs (Fig. 2.17). I have observed no association between beardlessness and spurlessness.

A gobbler may have a spur on one leg but not the other. Joe Slaton sent such a specimen taken in California. Some gobblers might have one spur that is much smaller than the other (Fig. 2.18). Deformed spurs are also seen. Sometimes deformed spurs are bilateral (both spurs) and sometimes not (only a single one).

Two spurs on each leg are rare—fewer than two dozen cases are known in male turkeys from Arkansas, Alabama, Florida, Minnesota, North Carolina, New York, Texas, West Virginia, and Wisconsin. Five double-spurred gobblers have been reported over a period of twenty years by hunters in Wakulla and Leon counties, Florida. A gobbler taken in Texas had two spurs on one leg and a single spur on the other (*Turkey Call*, July/August 1994). A similar specimen was taken in Wisconsin by Jerry Davis. A specimen taken by James Lambert in North Carolina had two spurs on each leg and also had two beards. Another specimen with double spurs and two beards was taken by Ronnie Williams in Arkansas.

When gobblers have double spurs, the extra one appears to be the lower and is usually smaller. In a few cases, both spurs are of similar size.

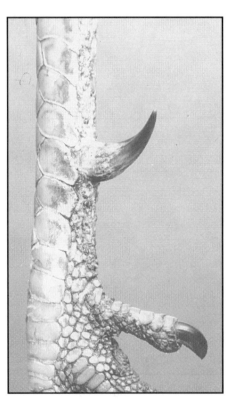

Fig. 2.19. *Spur abnormally hooked*

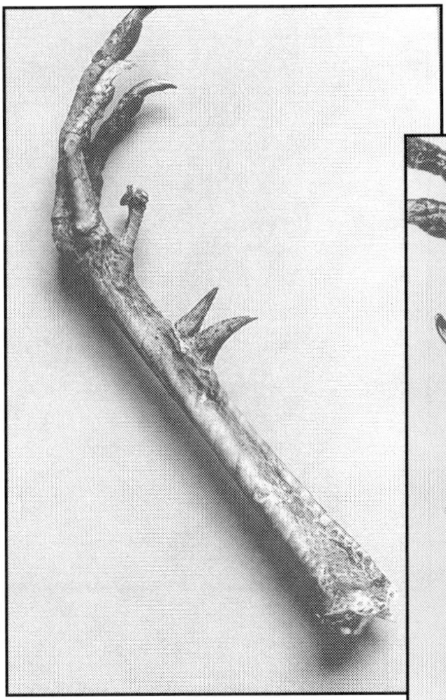

Fig. 2.20. Double spurs:
*A) of a specimen found dead
(left);*

B) another good example

Fig. 2.21. Triple spurs—the only case I know of

Fig. 2.22. Double spurs:
A) with spur caps (right);

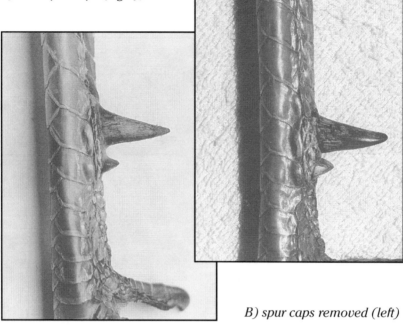

B) spur caps removed (left)

Fig. 2.23. False double spurs. There is no bone core under what appears to be the extra spur.

An extinct turkey, *Meleagris tridens*, known only from fossils, had three spurs on one leg. A living gobbler with three spurs on each leg (Fig. 2.21) was recently taken in Mississippi by Austin Lossett. It is the first triple-spurred living turkey I have heard about.

Extra spurs have bony cores like normal spurs (Fig. 2.22). I took one specimen in Florida that had what would appear to be a double spur (Fig. 2.23) but upon close examination, it was seen to be a kind of splinter growth on the bottom of the spur cap of the otherwise normal spur. The extra point had no bony core.

Hens with leg spurs have been reported from Florida, Texas, and Pennsylvania (specimen sent by Milford Kyler). About two percent of Florida hens have a spur on one or both legs. The longest hen spur I have seen measured about three-quarters of an inch and was sharp-pointed but not curved. The spurs of one hen specimen I dissected were not connected to the leg bone.

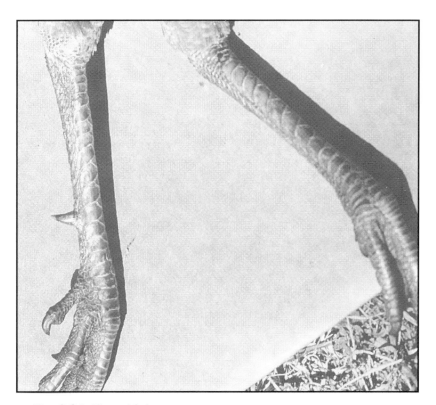

Fig. 2.24. *Hen with leg spur*

Spur growth is dependent on genetic factors and not on male hormones. This is supported by observations of a wild hen with a spur that nested successfully in a Florida study (Williams and Austin, 1988). If male hormones had been responsible for her spur, she could not have laid eggs or carried on the normal incubating processes. Except for the leg spur, she had all the physical features of a normal hen.

Toes and toenails

A gobbler taken in North Carolina in 1980 by Jimmy Womble had toenails unlike any ever before reported. At the time the

Fig. 2.25. Feet with "corkscrew" nails

specimen was shot, the toenails of one foot were twisted together, like a corkscrew. When untwisted, the result was the configuration depicted in the photo (Fig. 2.25). Gene Seney sent a photo of a Michigan gobbler taken in 1992 with similar nails on one foot. Others have been reported from Virginia, Michigan, and Alabama.

A gobbler specimen with no toenails on either foot was taken in Georgia in 1993 by Billy Wilkenson, and another with no nails on his right foot but normal nails on the left was taken the next day by Wilkenson near the same place. Both specimens had spurs and were otherwise normal in appearance.

A Kansas hunter reported a jake that had an extra toe. A few gobblers with one or more toes missing have been reported. It is easy to imagine a gobbler losing a toe in a leghold steel trap or having one shot off with a rifle. A gobbler reported to have had no toes at all may have been that way from birth. He was observed in the wild as a jake and again about a year later.

"Bumblefoot" is an enlargement of a toe or other part of the foot caused by a slow-growing bacterial infection that usually does not completely debilitate a turkey. I have seen four cases in which the turkey limped as it walked.

Leg color

The normal color of an Eastern wild turkey's lower leg is red. I have examined several specimens taken in the southeastern U. S. and Florida that had white tarsi. Dissection of the specimens revealed that the tissue layer under the scales, which in a normal specimen would be red, was white in the white legs.

Injury

Some abnormalities result from injury, such as being shot. I have examined several mended wing and leg bones of wild turkeys. I have received several reports of turkeys with mended radius bones that were seen flying and walking normally before being shot.

A gobbler taken in Alabama was missing the lower half of one leg and a toe on the other foot (Anon. 1992, p. 5). The wound had healed and he was able to get around.

While trapping turkeys in Florida during the 1960s, we saw a particular gobbler that had more than half his tail removed. It had healed and he seemed to be in good health. He was a dominant bird and quite a sight when he strutted.

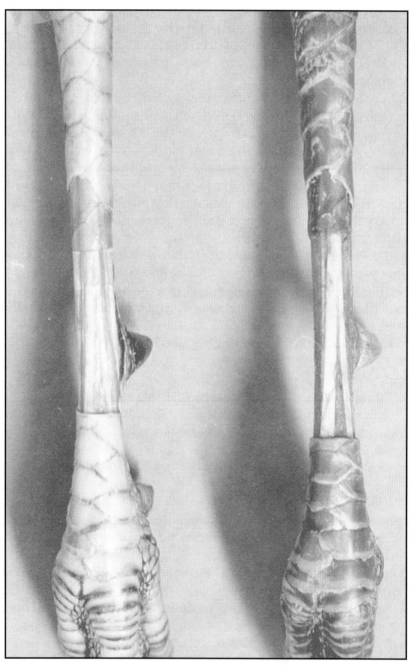

Fig. 2.26. *A white tarsus beside a normal one. A few of the leg scales have been lifted to show the difference in the color of the underlying tissue.*

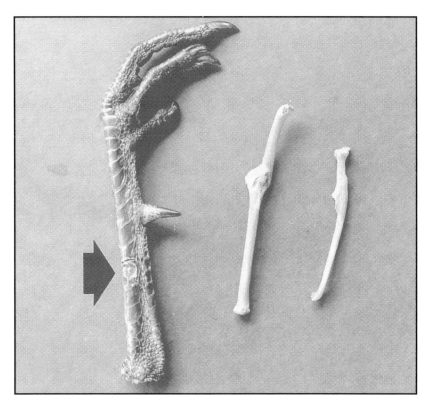

Fig. 2.27. *Lower leg, with an imbedded lead shot, and two mended wing bones*

I have found bird shot imbedded in the muscle of turkeys I took with a rifle. One gobbler had a No. 4 shot that had healed over in his tarsometatarsal bone and in another gobbler the joint between the tarsus and the tibiotarsus had an embedded No. 6 shot that fell out when I cut off his lower leg. Bird shot in old muscle wounds is common in turkeys taken on public hunting areas.

A few spurs have no spur cap—only the core of bone is present, the cap having been lost through injury.

Other Unusual Physical Conditions

Occasionally, the beak of a bird does not wear off properly at the tip and becomes excessively hooked as it continues to grow out of control. I have seen this in seagulls and a few other species of bird, but only once in a wild turkey (Fig. 2.28), taken in Florida and sent to me by Don Doughty. Perhaps even more strange is an adult gobbler reported by Dennis Baker that had no beak at all.

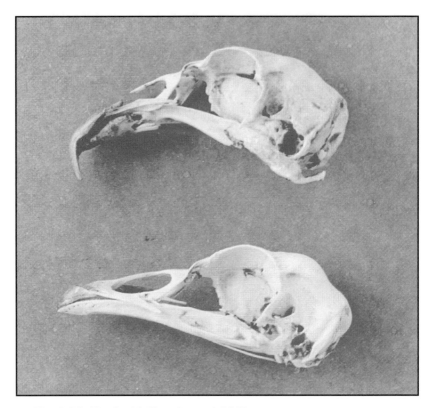

Fig. 2.28. Hooked bill and normal bill

A gobbler sometimes has no snood. I have seen human-imprinted wild and domestic turkeys whose snoods appeared to have been snipped off. I think this happens when young gobblers fight by grasping their opponent's snood in their beaks. In such cases, the tissue becomes enlarged where the snood was snipped (Fig. 2.29).

A snoodless specimen taken in Michigan was unusual in that there was no swelling at the snood's base (Kennamer, 1982). A Missouri gobbler had two well-developed snoods (Anon., 1983).

I examined a gobbler captured alive in Florida that had what I can only describe as an ossified head filoplume (Fig. 2.30). The one-half-inch-long length of bone-like material was growing from the head where a filoplume would normally have emerged. It appeared to have been broken off, suggesting that it may have been growing out continuously.

Hens normally have more head feathering than gobblers, but a hen turkey in Florida had a head that was completely feathered (Fig. 2.31).

Fig. 2.29. *Snoodless immature gobbler with swollen area where the snood would normally arise*

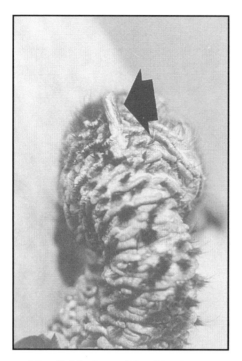

Fig. 2.30. *Bone-like filoplume on the head of a gobbler*

Gobblers have been seen in Alabama and North Carolina that had plumage growing from the tops of their heads, like crests. A mounted specimen (Fig. 2.32), taken by Bob Witte in Louisiana, was one of two crested gobblers seen there that same day. They were not running together.

Hen turkeys sometimes have gobbler plumage (Fig. 2.33). The condition was first reported by Edward A. McIlhenny (1914) from Texas and I have seen at least fourteen such specimens in Florida, both dead and alive. Randall Champ sent a color photograph of a juvenile hen in male plumage from West Virginia.

Male-plumaged hens have fewer small head and neck feathers than normal hens, but are of normal body size with normal female body proportions.

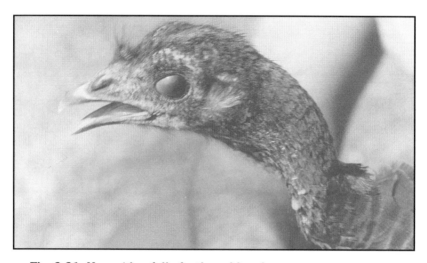

Fig. 2.31. *Hen with a fully feathered head*

A hen mounted by taxidermist Ben Skiles that won the "People's Choice" category in the 1995 NWTF Grand Nationals Wild Turkey Taxidermy contest had such plumage (see color section). She also had a beard. When I asked a few spectators at the show whether they saw anything unusual about the hen on display, only one commented that her plumage was unusual, but all noticed the beard. I suspect that gobbler-plumaged hen specimens are often overlooked.

How does a hen get gobbler plumage? It is known that hen plumage is produced by female hormones. If something should happen to the hen's gonads that caused their deterioration, her female hormone production would be curtailed and she would develop male-like plumage the next time she molted.

Fig. 2.32. *Gobbler specimen with plumes growing from the top of his head (Photo Bob Witte)*

I have dissected four gobbler-plumaged hens and found no ovary, only small remnants of oviducts and no organ resembling a male testis. Without ovaries, the hens were unable to produce the hormones required for development of female plumage. Since they do not have functional ovaries, hens with gobbler plumage cannot lay eggs.

If you see an off-color or other weird turkey specimen, you will usually find upon inquiry that similar specimens have been seen in the area before. That is because particular mutations tend to recur time and again in the same geographic areas. The freaks you see will not necessarily be the same individual reported before. If you shoot them, rest assured there'll eventually be another.

Recording Turkey Freaks

The abnormal physical conditions reported to me are listed in Table 2.1 with an estimate of their rarity. Not listed are a few unusual conditions that are not very rare or that were obviously caused by injury and disease.

Fig. 2.33. Hen with gobbler plumage (left) and a normal gobbler

Table 2.1. Unusual physical conditions in wild turkeys

Description	Reported frequently	Reported infrequently	Reported rarely	Reported very rarely
Plumage color				
Smoke gray	X			
Reddish marbling		X		
Red and white			X	
Reddish all over				X
1-2 wing feathers unbarred	X			
Most wing feathers unbarred				X
White wing blotches	X			
Speckled plumage				X
Complete albino plumage				X
Black plumage				X
Hen with gobbler type plumage			X	
Aberrant molting				
Round tail in juvenile	X			
Adult-type speculum			X	
Premature molt of juvenile	X			
Indented middle tail				X
Jake-like tail on gobbler				X
Uneven tail margin of adult			X	
20 tail feathers			X	
19 or 21 tail feathers				X
Beard				
Multiple beards	X			
Beardless gobblers	X			
Flawed zone, broken off[a]		X		
Blond color[b]		X		
Legs and feet				
Gobbler missing 1 or both spurs		X		
Double spur on 1 leg only				X
Double spurs on both legs				X
Hen with spur on 1 or both legs				X
Toenails missing				X
Toenails corkscrew-shaped			X	

[a] Flawed zone is without appreciable melanin; beard may be broken off at that point.

[b] Beard partially or wholly without appreciable melanin; beard not broken off.

Description	Reported frequently	Reported infrequently	Reported rarely	Reported very rarely
1 or more toes missing completely				X
1 or more extra toes				X
White lower legs	X			
Spur with cap missing				X
Broken bones healed			X	
Hooked bill				X
2 snoods				X
Snood missing				X
Hen's head fully feathered				X
Plumes on head				X
Ossified (bone-like) filoplume				X

Hunters who take turkeys with features of interest should have them recorded by reporting them to the National Wild Turkey Federation, to active turkey biologists, and to editors of turkey hunting magazines. It would be good to have the specimens mounted whole and well photographed. At least save and carefully photograph the body parts that are abnormal. Be sure to record the date and location where the specimen was taken on the back of a photograph, on the base of the mount, or put a small tag on the specimen.

Freak conditions may be of interest to natural history museums. Paleontologists should be particularly interested in knowing more about the wide spectrum of abnormal conditions that occur in animal skeletons so they won't jump to conclusions when they find an odd fossil. The "Three Spurred Turkey" *Meleagris tridens* (Wetmore, 1931) was once thought to be a new extinct species, but may have been only a freak. If you know anybody associated with a university zoology department or museum, check with them before you eat a freak.

I keep a file on turkey freaks and would like to learn about anything out of the ordinary, especially conditions I have not mentioned. As more data are obtained I will be able to report the frequency of freak conditions with better accuracy.

3

Grand Slam Hunting

The expression "grand slam," so widely used in hunting and other sports, originally referred to winning all the tricks in one hand in the card game of Bridge. As applied to turkey hunting, you have made a grand slam when you take the four subspecies of wild turkey that occur in the U. S. When you take also the Gould's, you have a royal slam. Add the Ocellated turkey and you have a world slam. It is not necessary to take the different subspecies in the same year, nor is there any requirement as to the sex of the specimens in order to make a "slam," only that they are taken legally.

Table 3.1. Wild turkey grand slamming definitions[a]

To make a–		
Grand Slam	**Royal Slam**	**World Slam**
...you take these subspecies–		
Eastern	Eastern	Eastern
Florida	Florida	Florida
Rio Grande	Rio Grande	Rio Grande
Merriam's	Merriam's	Merriam's
	Gould's	Gould's
		Ocellated

[a] *Turkey Call* magazine, p. 5, January-February 1988.

Since the grand slam concept is based on the subspecies of wild turkey, a few words are in order about species and subspecies.

Classification of the Turkey

Species and *subspecies* are biological classification terms. Different species of animal or plant are not very closely related. Put two separate species together, such as a male horse and a female cow, and they will not cross.

There are two separate species of turkey in the world today—the wild turkey of North America and the smaller Ocellated turkey of southern Mexico and Central America. Both species evolved in the Western Hemisphere; no species of turkey has ever occurred naturally in any other part of the world.

Subspecies, or races, are subdivisions of the same species and are closely related, much like varieties of domestic animals. Two breeds of cattle will interbreed. So will two subspecies of wild turkey if you put them together. That is why no subspecies can occur within the geographic range of another—they must be isolated from each other or they would interbreed, producing mongrels. The populations would merge and the distinctiveness of the populations would vanish. The reason wild turkey subspecies breed "true" is because only their own kind is available to them for mating. Geography is the usual isolating factor. Thus a wild animal subspecies is as much a geographic phenomenon as it is a genetic one.

Table 3.2. Classification of wild turkey

Classification category	Scientific name	Common name	Number in world
Class	Aves	Birds	8900
Order	Galliformes	Fowl-like birds	259
Family	Phasianidae	Pheasants	179
Subfamily	Meleagridinae	Turkeys	2
Genus	Meleagris	Turkeys	2
Species	gallopavo	Wild turkey	1
Subspecies	silvestris	Eastern wild turkey	1
	osceola	Florida wild turkey	1
	intermedia	Rio Grande wild turkey	1
	merriami	Merriam's wild turkey	1
	mexicana	Gould's wild turkey	1

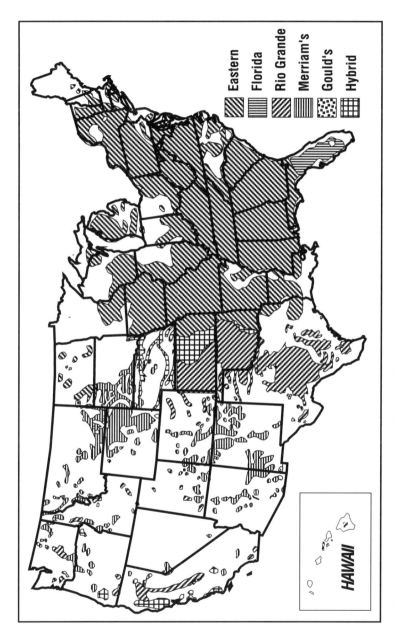

Fig. 3.1. Present distribution of the wild turkey subspecies in the U.S. See Fig. 3.11 for the intergrade zone between the Florida and Easten subspecies.

Turkeys were domesticated in Mexico between two thousand and four thousand years ago and carried to Europe by Spanish explorers in the 1500s. Domestic turkeys later got to the American colonies from Europe. The wild turkey in the U. S. has never been domesticated.

Turkeys are classified in the family with the pheasants (Steadman, 1980). The turkey's scientific name is *Meleagris gallopavo*. The first term, *Meleagris*, is the name of the genus the turkey belongs to, *gallopavo* is the species. The scientific name of the Ocellated turkey is *Meleagris ocellata*. The relationship between the wild turkey (*Meleagris gallopavo*) and the Ocellated turkey (*Meleagris ocellata*) is similar to the relationship between the coyote (*Canis latrans*) and the wolf (*Canis lupus*).

The present distribution of the wild turkey subspecies (Fig. 3.1) has been affected by transfers of wild stock, making it difficult to identify the subspecies involved in some places. Wild turkey populations now exist in parts of the U. S. where none existed before.

Early efforts were commonly made to establish turkey populations in other parts of the world by releasing domestic turkeys, but all failed except on a few islands. Island survival is possible because of the absence or relative ineptness of predator populations on islands. Even unfit prey species, such as domestic turkeys, can survive if the local predators can't catch them.

When domestic stock successfully goes wild, the resulting populations are called "feral." Examples of feral animals on the U. S. mainland are the domestic pigeon, horse, burro, and wild pig. There are no feral turkeys in North or South America, but there are feral populations in New Zealand, Hawaii, and on some other islands.

Transplants of wild-trapped turkeys made in Europe in recent years have been only marginally successful. For an account of stocking done outside the New World, see Wunz (1992). Wild turkeys would likely do well in many parts of the world if wild-trapped stock were released.

Some scientists believe that the Merriam's wild turkey was derived from captive turkeys that escaped from American Indians five hundred to one thousand years ago. If that is so, the Merriam's wild turkey could be technically considered a feral population. That will be discussed later.

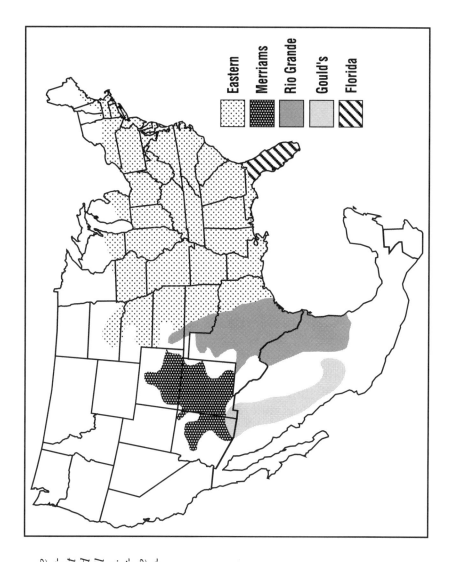

Fig. 3.2. Range of the wild turkey subspecies before European settlement of North America. Adapted from Aldrich and Duvall (1955) and other sources. See Fig. 3.11 for the intergrade zone between the Florida and Eastern subspecies.

Eastern
Merriams
Rio Grande
Gould's
Florida

To label a modern turkey population established by transplanting outside the original range of the turkey as one or another of the five subspecies should be done only when a single subspecies has been used to stock the new range and when it can be shown that contemporary specimens there closely match the physical description of the subspecies being claimed.

Would a hunter who goes for a Merriam's or Rio Grande turkey in California, where both subspecies have been successfully established, be grand slam hunting? Not in my book. More about that later.

Since subspecies are geographic in nature, the best way to know where to hunt them is to refer to reliable range maps. Pay particular attention to the maps in Figures 3.1 and 3.2. In a few places the subspecies that originally occurred has been replaced by another subspecies through stocking. Rio Grande populations now occur in former Merriam's range in the Rocky Mountains and in former Eastern range in Oklahoma and Kansas. Merriam's and hybrids now occur in Nebraska and South Dakota where Easterns formerly occurred.

Physical features can be used to distinguish the subspecies. There are small differences that only a trained eye would notice, but also a few differences that any hunter can apply with confidence.

I have visited the U. S. National Museum, American Museum of Natural History, and a few other large museums to see their scientific collections and have also examined freshly killed specimens of all five turkey subspecies. The following descriptions are based on a study of the scientific literature and my examination of specimens.

Eastern wild turkey (Meleagris gallopavo silvestris)

The term *silvestris*, which designates the Eastern subspecies, means "of the woodlands." It was named in 1817 based on Pennsylvania specimens. At that time, the eastern wild turkey occupied a vast range from the Atlantic Ocean to the Great Plains.

The upper tail coverts and tail margin of silvestris are tipped with brown (see color section). These markings are of a slightly lighter shade in young specimens and there is much variability in tail color even among adults.

Fig. 3.3. Primary wing feathers of an Eastern wild turkey: A) whole wing

Silvestris shares brown tail margin coloration with the Florida turkey (see below). The tail margin of silvestris is usually lighter in shade than osceola's when typical specimens are compared directly, but when a large number of osceola and silvestris is compared, overlap in tail color is evident.

The secondary wing feathers of silvestris have prominent white bars and are edged in white, producing a conspicuous whitish triangular area on each side of the back in standing turkeys when the wings are closed.

Distinguishing silvestris from the others. The brown tail tip of the Eastern and Florida subspecies easily distinguish them from the Rio Grande, Merriam's, and Gould's which have white or nearly white tail margins.

B) close-up view

Fig. 3.4. Eastern gobblers showing strong black and white wing barring pattern

Fig. 3.5. Primary wing feathers of a Florida wild turkey: A) dark example;

The Eastern and Florida subspecies are distinguished from each other by the difference in the black and white barring of the primary wing feathers. The Eastern subspecies has white wing bars of width equal to the black bars and the white extends across the entire feather (Figs. 3.3). In the Florida subspecies, the white wing bars are narrower than the black and are broken; few, if any, extend all the way across the primary wing feathers.

B) lighter colored example

Florida wild turkey (Meleagris gallopavo osceola)

The Florida subspecies was named in 1890 in honor of a famous nineteenth century Seminole Indian. The first specimens came from near Tarpon Springs. The Florida wild turkey occurs only in the peninsula of Florida.

Fig. 3.6. *Florida gobblers showing dark wings with weak white barring*

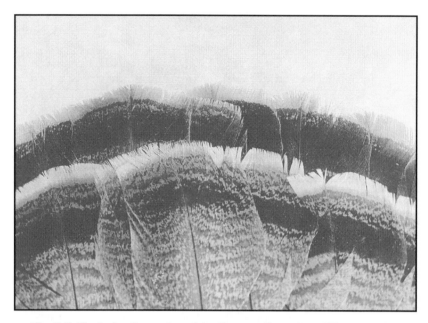

Fig. 3.7. *Typical tail margins of the Eastern (lower) and Florida turkeys*

The Florida turkey is of smaller average skeletal size and body weight than any other turkey subspecies, but large Florida specimens are larger than small examples of the other subspecies. Twenty-pound Florida spring gobblers are not rare. Neither are healthy fourteen pounders.

Distinguishing osceola from the others. Osceola is distinguished from the three western subspecies by its brown tail margin (versus their whitish tail margins), which it has in common with silvestris. Osceola is distinguished from silvestris by the dark barring of its wing feathers (Fig. 3.5) as previously mentioned.

The secondary wing feathers of osceola are also dark and, when the wing is folded, the light-colored triangular patch on the back is not as noticeable as it is in silvestris.

Rio Grande wild turkey (Meleagris gallopavo intermedia)

The Rio Grande turkey is a bird of the arid southwestern U. S. and northeastern Mexico. It was named in 1892 based on specimens from Hidalgo County, Texas. The name *intermedia* reflects the opinion of the zoologist who named the subspecies that it is intermediate in appearance between the two eastern and two western mountain subspecies and indeed, in many ways it is.

Fig. 3.8. Rio Grande turkey primary wing feathers. Note the gray shading in the white bars and the similarity to osceola.

Distinguishing Rio Grande from the others. The best way to distinguish a Rio Grande specimen is by the color of the tail margin and of the outer edge of the other large tail feathers (see color section). Its tail margin is much lighter in shade than the medium brown of the Florida or Eastern turkeys and distinctly darker than the same feathers in the Merriam's and Gould's.

The primary and secondary wing feathers of the Rio Grande turkey (Fig. 3.8) are not as dark as the Florida turkey nor as whitish as the Eastern.

Merriam's wild turkey (Meleagris gallopavo merriami)

The Merriam's is a bird of the ponderosa pine foothills of the southern U. S. Rocky Mountains. The subspecies was named in honor of the western zoologist C. Hart Merriam from specimens taken in Veracruz, Mexico. It occurs now only in the U. S.

Merriam's has been successfully stocked north of its natural range in the Rockies, in the Pacific states, east of the mountains in Nebraska, and in some other places in the Northwest.

Some adult Merriam's turkeys have legs that appear more brown colored than other turkeys. I have dissected the legs of two Merriam's adult gobblers from Colorado and found the same red pigment layer as seen in the other subspecies. Apparently, the red layer is sometimes masked by dark pigmentation in the leg scales even of adult specimens.

Recent archeological and paleotological evidence (Rea, 1980) suggests that the Merriam's turkey is descended from stock the early Indians of Mexico raised in captivity. The captive variety is called "Large Indian Domestic" (McKusick, 1980) and is known only from remains found in caves and diggings.

According to the paleontological record, there were no wild turkey populations in the southern U. S. Rocky Mountains before the Indians got there a few thousand years ago. The Indians got turkeys from Mexico, and their captive birds were the only turkeys in the southern Rocky Mountains. Evidently, some of the captive stock escaped and became the wild Merriam's turkey. This is supported in that skeletal and other physical features of wild Merriam's match those of the "Large Indian Domestic."

Early American Indians would not have domesticated wild animals as thoroughly as we do today, and the turkeys they kept captive may have not suffered the severe genetic reductions that modern breeds of captive animals do. The Indians may have discovered parental imprinting and could have been rearing turkeys that were on the edge of wildness.

There is no agreement among the experts about the origin of the captive Indian strain in Mexico (and therefore modern Merriam's wild turkeys). The Large Indian Domestic strain died out when the Indian culture did in that region five hundred to one thousand years ago. The only known living survivors are the turkeys we know today as Merriam's wild turkey of the southern Rocky Mountains.

Distinguishing Merriam's from the others. Both the Merriam's and Gould's have white margins on the feathers of the lower back and tail, and that distinguishes them from the Eastern and Florida subspecies, which have brown tail margins, and from the Rio Grande, which has tan. I have seen no overlap between the whiteness of the tail margin of the Rio Grande with the two mountain subspecies Gould's and Merriam's.

Merriam's and Gould's look much alike. Identifying a specimen is no problem if you know where the specimen came from, since the Merriam's and Gould's do not overlap in range.

The tail margin of many Merriam's specimens is not quite as pure white, nor is the white rim as wide as in a typical Gould's specimen, but there are some very white-tailed Merriam's turkeys, and there is much overlap in this trait between the two subspecies. Using this trait, you may occasionally misidentify a Merriam's as a Gould's. You would be less likely to think a true Gould's is a Merriam's.

I have detected a few differences between Gould's and Merriam's in plumage markings, but need to look at more specimens before I write about it. In the meantime, I suggest you use the maps (Figs. 3.1 and 3.2), taking into account that some range formerly occupied only by Merriam's has been stocked with Rios and hybrids.

If you are examining a specimen of unknown origin and are not certain whether it is a Gould's or Merriam's, look at the lower legs— the lower legs of a Merriam's gobbler are shorter than six inches and do not have noticeable black pigment in the toes; even the shortest lower legs of Gould's gobblers and spring jakes are longer than six inches and the toes are nearly black.

Fig. 3.9. *Primary wing feathers of Merriam's wild turkey. Note the gray shading in the white barring of the middle primaries.*

Gould's wild turkey (Meleagris gallopavo mexicana)

The Gould's turkey is a bird of the mountains and oak-pine foothills of northwestern Mexico. The original museum specimens were taken in 1856 by a zoologist named Gould, and his name has become the vernacular name for the subspecies, although I think "Mexican wild turkey" would be more appropriate.

Distinguishing Gould's from the others. The tips of the upper tail coverts and of the largest tail feathers are pure white in most specimens of the Gould's. In this respect it resembles many specimens of the Merriam's, as discussed above. Leg length and color are the best way to distinguish specimens of these two subspecies, also discussed above.

The width of the outer white tail band depends to some extent on the season the bird is taken. By late spring, some of the white edge has worn off and the band is slightly narrower than it was in fall, especially the middle tail feathers. Look at the outer feathers, not the middle feathers, to see the true width of the white band. The white margins of the upper tail coverts also wear appreciably and tend to curl up on the edges by late spring. That applies also to the Merriam's and Rio Grande.

Fig. 3.10. Primary wing feathers of Gould's wild turkey with gray shading in the white barring of the primaries, similar to the Merriam's and Rio Grande

The reason tail wear is so pronounced in Merriam's, Gould's, and Rio Grande is that the white parts of feathers contain no melanin to strengthen them and they simply wear out.

There are a few other differences about the Gould's. It is the largest of the turkey subspecies in both skeleton size and body weight. Its lower legs and feet are immense. I have measured tracks in Mexico with middle toes more than four inches long. A four-inch middle toe would be monstrous for an Eastern turkey; three and one-half inches would be a record for the Florida turkey.

Gould's turkeys have more black pigment in their lower legs than any other subspecies, especially in the toes. Upon dissection, the underlying pigment layer of a Gould's' lower legs is as red as in any of the other subspecies. We know that melanin adds strength to leg scales, and I suspect that the black in the toe scales of the Gould's is there to protect the toes from the rocks that abound in the soil where the turkey lives.

There are inaccurate statements in the literature that the Gould's is a short-legged turkey. It is true that the ratio of lower leg (tarsus) length to wing length is smaller in Gould's than in the other subspecies (Stangel et al. 1992) but the absolute length of the lower legs of the Gould's is greater than any other turkey subspecies. I confirmed that by examining the skeletons of thirteen recently taken gobblers in the mountains of Chihuahua in 1994 and 1995.

The body plumage of the Gould's is sometimes said to have a bluish-green coloration, but that is not usually noticeable under field conditions. Turkey plumage color depends on light reflections. The one hundred or more Gould's wild turkeys I have seen alive and the thirteen freshly killed I have handled were no greener than the other subspecies.

Planning Your Grand Slam

Some people think you have to take your turkeys in the same year to accomplish a grand slam. Not so. When you take the four subspecies that occur in the U. S., in the range where they naturally live, you have made a grand slam. Take also the Gould's and you have a royal slam.

For annual summaries of hunting regulations in various states, check the fall and winter issues of turkey hunting magazines, especially *Turkey Call* and *Turkey & Turkey Hunting*. Contact the National Wild Turkey Federation, P.O. Box 530, Edgefield, SC 29824 to subscribe to *Turkey Call.* Write Krause Publications, 700 East State Street, Iola, WI 54990-0001 for *Turkey & Turkey Hunting.* Other magazine publishers have special turkey hunting editions with useful information about hunting in different places. Watch for them on the newsstands in winter.

To avoid dating this account with information that will change, I have listed the sources of hunting regulations for each state (Appendix).

Most state wildlife agencies set their hunting regulations in the spring or early summer. Write the state wildlife agency for current regulations. Ask about buying your license and permits by mail, about any restrictions on non-resident turkey hunters, and whether you have to have a hunting license to apply for special quota hunts on public areas.

Mexican law requires non-resident hunters to use licensed outfitters, who are in turn required by law to enter a contract with the hunter and perform certain services. If you plan to hunt in Mexico, check with an established outfitter about current regulations there. Hunting regulations in Mexico are made on a year to year basis, as in most states, and there is no guarantee what they will be until they are made.

If you book with an outfitter you do not already know, obtain references and speak with him by phone. If you have any doubt about an outfitter, check further or try another.

I am not aware of any important differences in hunting technique for the different subspecies—what works for one will work for the others. Their voices are not identical, but are similar, and their food habits depend only on what's available to eat. The essence of hunting the different wild turkey subspecies is in the landscapes you hunt and in the people you hunt with. New places, new faces, different kinds of trees and wildlife, and new experiences create appeal that rewards the turkey hunter who travels.

Going for the Eastern

The Eastern subspecies is the most widely distributed of the five wild turkey subspecies and consequently is the most available for hunting.

Silvestris is closely identified with the eastern deciduous forest—where oaks, maples, hickories, and beech turn color and shed their leaves in fall. It occupies the most diverse landscapes of any subspecies—coastal swamps similar to osceola range, river

Fig. 3.16. *A cypress swamp of the kind that occurs in southern lowlands of the Eastern and Florida wild turkey range*

Fig. 3.17. *Managed southern pine and hardwoods forest landscape of the Eastern wild turkey range*

Fig. 3.18. Spring hardwoods in the Eastern wild turkey's range

bottoms, eastern mountains, farms, hardwoods, large woodlots, hemlock, pinewoods—you name it. It lives from the subtropics of the Deep South to southern Canada, and from the wettest wetlands of the low country of the Atlantic coast to the driest forests of the midwest. If the landscape has woods, Eastern turkeys can live there, and thanks to recent restoration programs, they probably do.

If you haven't hunted silvestris but plan to, you can get a good flavor of early day eastern turkey hunting from Henry Davis' *The American Wild Turkey.* Davis was a sportsman and attorney who hunted the South Carolina low country when turkeys were scarce and getting scarcer. There are many books about hunting Eastern wild turkeys written by contemporary authors.

Fig. 3.19. Fall hardwoods in the Eastern wild turkey's range

Going for the Florida

The Florida turkey is the only turkey subspecies that occurs in only a single state. It is also unique in having a zone where it intergrades with another subspecies. That raises a question: To which subspecies do you assign specimens from the Florida/ Eastern intergrade zone? Are they either? Neither? Or both? The National Wild Turkey Federation classifies turkeys in the intergrade zone (Fig. 3.11) as silvestris for their record-keeping purposes.

The physical features that characterize silvestris (i. e. prominent white barring in the wings) become more pronounced in specimens as you go northward from southern Florida, but you will not find typical silvestris specimens south of the middle of South Carolina, Georgia, Alabama, or Mississippi. The most practical solution for your osceola quest is to hunt south of the Suwannee River in Florida. Consider turkeys of northern Florida and those in adjoining states near the Florida state line to be silvestris for grand slam hunting purposes, as does the NWTF.

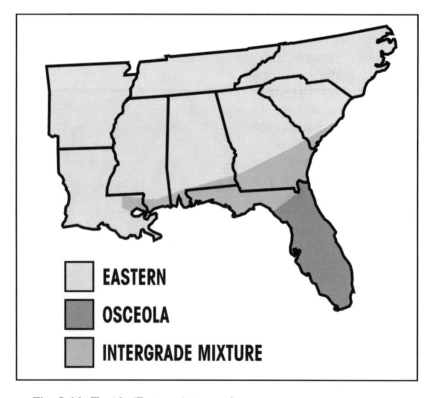

Fig. 3.11. Florida/Eastern intergrade zone

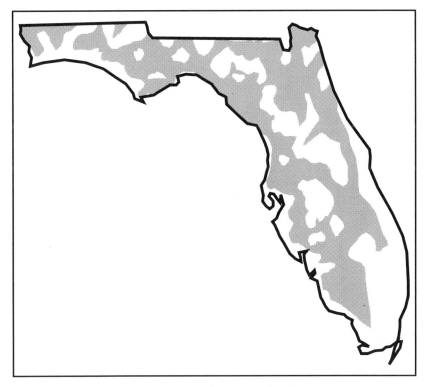

Fig. 3.12. Present range of the Florida wild turkey

Because osceola occurs only in Florida, and since Florida has become the fourth most populated state in the U. S. (and isn't as big as Texas to begin with), finding a place to hunt the osceola is no easy feat.

The growth of human civilization around most urban parts of Florida, combined with agriculture and silviculture, have shrunk the habitat available to wild turkeys. Fortunately, much of Florida's human population is packed along the coastlines where it has not as seriously impacted wild turkey habitat as it might otherwise have.

Florida was the first state to finish its turkey restoration effort and there are good turkey populations in Florida wherever there is habitat. No part of the peninsula can be singled out as better than any other. The only counties with too few turkeys to hunt are in the Everglades at the southern tip of the state, where there never has been many turkeys. The Everglades is a marsh with little dry land and too little timber for turkeys except in a few dry spots of the Big Cypress Swamp.

Fig. 3.13. *Florida landscape showing patchy cover types*

Florida has an extensive public hunting land program but the "Wildlife Management Areas" are heavily hunted. The state wildlife agency and other land management agencies that sponsor public hunting in Florida will be going to more limited-access public hunting as conditions become more crowded on public areas. Ask about "quota" spring turkey hunts when you check with the agency.

Fig. 3.14. Inside a Florida hammock

Wild turkey populations are good on many large Florida cattle ranches and woodland properties where they are conservatively hunted. If you have the opportunity to hunt on a Florida ranch, you won't do any better than that.

Much private hunting land in Florida is being leased to hunting clubs, but there are a few private hunting guides that offer turkey hunting for a fee. I have a hunting camp at Fisheating Creek in Glades County where we offer trip-hunting. To contact the camp, call (941) 675-4117 or write Fisheating Creek Hunting Camp, P. O. Box 117, Palmdale, FL 33944. Watch also the classified ads in "Where to Hunt" sections of turkey hunting magazines.

Hunting the osceola is like hunting the Eastern wild turkey except the climate is warmer, the landscape is flat and sometimes wet, the cover is denser, and even the broadleaf vegetation is mostly evergreen.

Cover types are patchy in Florida—if you walk a straight line, you won't go far before you hit a different cover type and sooner or later you'll be wading. Shallow water is not a barrier to Florida turkeys—they will walk through water up to a foot deep and fly over deeper water. Although turkeys are tolerant of dense cover in Florida, they avoid especially dense low vegetation such as solid stands of saw palmetto.

Variable cover types in small patches make excellent wild turkey habitat. That makes it unnecessary for turkeys to travel far to get what they need, so their home ranges are correspondingly small.

Young cabbage palm trees, thin stands of saw palmetto, and other low shrubs provide good hiding places for hunters. Portable hunting blinds are much less important than in other turkey ranges. Camouflage clothing is widely worn but not as critical in Florida as in the eastern deciduous woodlands.

Florida is relatively warm in spring, but in the northern part of the state, be prepared for the possibility of near-freezing weather at sunup in late fall and midday highs in the 80s toward the end of the spring hunting season. It can be wet and you may need a change of boots. Knee-high rubber boots are a good idea. Inquire about water levels a few days before your Florida hunt.

Snake bite is no problem in Florida. There are more rattlesnakes in Texas. In Florida you stand a better chance of getting struck by lightning or shot in a robbery attempt than being snake bitten. And alligators eat only about one person per year. The more serious hazards are mosquitoes and poison ivy.

If you haven't hunted in Florida, but plan to, you might want to read my book *The Art and Science of Wild Turkey Hunting.*

Fig. 3.15. *Inside a Florida creek swamp*

Fig. 3.20. Rio Grande turkey range in Texas—cactus in foreground, mesquite in background (Photo Wyman Meinzer)

Going for the Rio Grande

The Rio Grande wild turkey is a bird of the arid lands of southern Oklahoma, Texas, and eastern Mexico. It lives with roadrunners and coyotes among the cactus and mesquite.

For many years, the Eastern wild turkey usurped the image of "the wild turkey." Books and magazines said that the way to tell a wild turkey from a tame one is to look at its tail—wild turkeys were supposed to have dark brown tail margins while domestic turkeys had revealing white tail margins. That is not quite true—the two western mountain wild turkey subspecies, Merriam's and Gould's, have white tail margins and the Rio Grande's tail margin is sometimes nearly white.

It's risky to generalize about Rio range, especially Texas, but I will anyway. Where the Rios are, many things will either bite you or stick you, so wear good boots and be careful where you sit. Many of the streams run dry except when it's raining, so carry drinking water. Sometimes there is no place to hide, so wear camo.

The water that exists is often in water holes made for cattle and sheep, and that may be where the turkeys are. The landscape is wide, open, and big. Range that looks like a desert one season will become a green and grassy meadow when it has rained. There is not enough rain over the long term to grow many trees, so you and the turkeys can see each other a long way. Unless you use binoculars and look first, the turkeys have a way of evading you at long distances.

Rifles are often used in Rio Grande country because the open country gives the rifleman advantages he does not have in heavier cover of the East. A combination shotgun/rifle is a good weapon for Rios, but your faithful old turkey shotgun is completely adequate. If you use a rifle and plan to mount your bird whole, or hope to eat most of it, you will need to use downloaded ammunition to ballistics near that of the .22 Hornet. Standard high power rifle factory loads will blow a turkey apart. Best to use your shotgun.

Rio Grande turkeys may move great distances daily and tend to come from all around to roost in the same trees every night. Roosts are often along creek beds or a few other places where there are trees. Any kind of tree will do, including mesquite, and they don't have to be very big. Rio Grandes are even known to roost on fences and power lines in areas where there are few or no trees.

Fig. 3.21. *Rio Grande turkey range in Texas with a man-made water source (Photo James Dickson)*

There are many commercial hunting outfitters and guides in Rio Grande country. Rio hunting is also available in Mexico (Fig. 3.1).

You can read about hunting the Rio Grande in *The Turkey Hunter's Digest* by Oklahoman Dwain Bland. Bland is a widely traveled guide and a good observer. In the book he discusses hunting the other subspecies too.

Going for the Merriam's

The Merriam's is a bird of the Rocky Mountains and the foothills and canyons of the southwestern U. S. It has been successfully transplanted throughout much of the hilly Northwest. It is noted for its movement up and down mountains with changes of the seasons. It can move a long way horizontally too—as far as it has to for feeding, roosting, watering, and other necessities of life. When pickings are lean, Merriam's will vacate a place where it was abundant in better times.

Merriam's turkeys are known to visit farms to find waste grain and handouts, especially in cold winter weather. They may seem rather tame in such situations, but most live far from human habitation and there is nothing tame about them.

Fig. 3.22. *Merriam's wild turkey range in Colorado (Photo Butch Austin)*

In the Rocky Mountains you could wind up hunting spring gobblers in a snowstorm, as I once did in Montana. A light snow was falling at daylight that early May morning. We had to use chains on the truck and almost didn't get there.

Soon after I got settled, a big-footed old bird gobbled on the roost. He responded to my yelping but wouldn't come my way. As I heard him moving away, I was able to find where he flew down in the fresh snow. (That's how I knew he had big feet.) I had always wanted to track a turkey in snow.

The gobbler was alone and moving steadily. I followed within hearing distance. When I gained on him, his tracks were clean; if I fell behind, I would almost lose them in the falling snow. He gobbled from time to time, but my best yelping couldn't turn him.

After I could see that he was not going to turn back, I decided to cut under a cliff along a creek and get ahead of him. I had to move double time to do it but finally I got ahead and got ready. I heard him gobble again and could tell he was still coming.

As I waited, it stopped snowing. He quit gobbling. I waited an hour before giving him up. When I headed back, I found the story written in the snow: gobbler tracks in walking stride, then longer steps of a running turkey joined by the tracks of two coyotes. A few feet farther there were no more turkey tracks.

Fig. 3.23. *Another Merriam's turkey landscape in Colorado (Photo Butch Austin)*

The gobbler was airborne and away. At that point the coyotes' tracks turned back into the timber. As far as I know, the old gobbler is still out there dodging coyotes. I had to go back to Florida.

Merriam's turkeys are usually associated with open stands of ponderosa pine that run in size from large in the moist mountains to small in the dry foothills. Pine trees themselves are of little importance to the Merriam's—ponderosa merely characterizes the life zone where the turkey lives.

The Merriam's tends to have favorite roosting places in certain stands of large conifers, including ponderosa pine, but it is not as consistent in using the same trees as are the Rio Grande and Gould's (see below), probably because it has more options.

Much of the Merriam's' range is grazed by cattle, which is beneficial to turkey habitat if the forest is not abused, and there is much land available to public hunting on national forests and BLM lands. The Merriam's turkey is upstaged in the Rockies by big game mammals and is not heavily hunted.

Going for the Gould's

Gould's turkeys live in the Sierra Madre mountains of Mexico, mainly in the states of Chihuahua, Sonora, Sinaloa, and Durango (Fig. 3.1). Only a small population occurs in the U. S., near the U. S.-Mexico border (Potter, Schemnitz, and Zeedyk, 1985). It is considered an "endangered species" in the U. S. and is not hunted but is being stocked north of the border at this time. Although the extent of its range has been reduced over the years, Gould's is still abundant on private ranches in parts of Mexico.

The Gould's gobbler is called *cocono*; the hen is *cocona* and the young bird is *coconita*. Some other Mexican names for wild turkeys are *guajolote, totoe*, and *pipilo*.

The Gould's subspecies has not been well studied by zoologists or wildlife biologists and very little wildlife management, other than harvest management through governmental regulations, is practiced in Mexico. The Gould's turkey is potentially an important natural resource with great economic value to the people of Mexico.

The major range of the Gould's is about the same latitude as Florida, but the elevation ranges from about three thousand to

Fig. 3.24. Mountain scene in Gould's range of Chihuahua, Mexico

nine thousand feet above sea level, which, climate-wise, is equivalent to its being much farther north. Major Gould's gobbling occurs in late April and early May.

Fig. 3.25. David Austin shooting video of Gould's habitat in the Sierra Madre Mountains, Chihuahua, Mexico

There is likely to be morning frost in Gould's country, then that afternoon you may see short-sleeve weather. By sundown the hunting party will draw closer to the campfire and will sleep in winter sleeping bags with long johns. The weather can be very windy and the air is extremely dry.

In northern Mexico, the landscape at lower elevations is sparsely forested by eastern U. S. standards. There are several species of pine, but the prime timber was logged heavily many years ago and has been slow to regenerate in the arid climate and limited seed sources, especially in the foothills and at lower elevations. Cattle grazing may be a retarding factor too. The climate is wetter and cooler at higher elevations and more heavily forested with a wider variety of trees and shrubs.

Large Chihuahua and Apache pine trees are favorite Gould's turkey roosts, as indicated by the piles of droppings and feathers under favorite clumps of roost trees. The Gould's will roost in dead pines even when large live pines are nearby, and occasionally in other large trees such as sycamore.

You can quickly learn to spot suitable roost trees, and can confirm their use by checking for droppings, but turkeys do not use the same roosts every night and seasonal changes can be marked. Dropping accumulations under favorite roosts can be deceptive. The arid climate and wind will dry out a fresh dropping in a few hours and the dropping may last relatively unchanged for months after that.

Some of the foothills and low mountain slopes are covered in stands of blue oak, silverleaf oak, emory oak, and other small oak trees. The same species of oak will grow into large trees in moist soils near creeks and at high altitudes, but will remain dwarfed, windbeaten shrubs on a dry and windy mountainside.

Fig. 3.26. *Creek valley in Gould's range at 6,000 feet elevation*

Even small oak trees bear heavy crops of acorns in fall. You can find scratchings done last winter under the oaks, even in late spring. The toenails of the turkeys are badly worn from scratching for acorns.

The courses of permanent creeks are marked by sycamores and several other large hardwood trees, including black walnut and cottonwood poplar. Junipers of several species are everywhere, especially below about six thousand feet. Junipers, piñon pine, and walnut produce important fall and winter turkey foods.

The variety and vigor of vegetation increase at higher altitudes, in ravines, and on north slopes because of better moisture conditions. Sugar maple and white pine come in at higher altitudes and oregano grows wild.

Grass leaves, dried grass seed heads, certain tubers such as wild onion, many kinds of succulent greenery, and various species of flowers are important spring turkey foods. I was admiring a yellow mountain columbine flower from my photo blind along a Chihuahua mountain stream in early May when a Gould's hen strolled by and ate it.

When you are making plans to hunt the Gould's, be sure to check with your outfitter about preparations. You can get normal supplies in Mexico, but not after leaving the main road. The soil will be rocky and you may find lugsoled boots advantageous. You will need binoculars and a small canteen for water. Drink bottled water and boil your cooking water—or you can use water purification equipment. Even the cleanest and coolest mountain stream may harbor Giardia, which can cause a serious case of diarrhea that will spoil your hunt.

If you know any Spanish, you will get a chance to practice it on your Mexican hunt. Most Mexican people who interact with Americans can speak some English, but if you don't know any Spanish, take an English/Spanish dictionary to look up a few essential words that you may need to communicate with your guides and cooks who know only Spanish.

Be sure your outfitter has scales to weigh your gobbler and, if there is no source of ice, be prepared to skin and preserve your trophy by taking borax, salt, and at least a little knowledge about what to do. (See Chapters 4 and 5.) If camping, you may want to carry one of the plastic bags from a camping supply store in order to heat bath water in the sun. Be sure your tent is pitched out of the wind and out of the direct sun.

Fig. 3.27. *Mountain stream in Gould's wild turkey range at 7,000 feet elevation*

You may have trouble getting your turkey specimen out of Mexico because of regulations of the U. S. Department of Agriculture. What you have to do is covered in Chapter 5.

There is presently no fall turkey hunting season in Mexico. The spring gobbler season usually runs from March or early April through the end of April or early May. The annual bag limit is one gobbler. Some of the out-fitters are requesting the government to set a later season to take advantage of what they think is better gobbling.

Prices for three- to five-day trips with rustic accommo-dations and minimal guiding assistance are $1,500 to $1,800 including hunting license. You will need a gun permit. Your outfitter can help you. Red tape rivals tortillas in omnipresence.

Fig. 3.28. Lolo, our Mexican camp cook, making a tortilla

There will be a few papers to fill out in advance. Here are some things your outfitter will tell you to provide:

• Current U. S. passport or passport type color photos for a tourist identification certificate and other papers requiring photos. Up to ten photos may be needed even if you already have a passport.

• Copy of your birth certificate.

• Letter from a physician on his business stationery stating that you have no serious contagious disease or mental problem so that you can get a visa and gun permit.

• Letter from your sheriff or police chief saying that you have no criminal history.

• Make, model, and serial number of the shotgun you plan to carry.

• Possibly some other details that your outfitter will know about.

Some outfitters recommend that you not bring military style camo clothing because of the political unrest that occurs in Mexico from time to time. You might be mistaken for an invader. Carry dark clothing or recreational camo patterns.

While in Mexico, you will see wild things with which you are not familiar, and you will find some interesting souvenirs. On a recent hunt I found a mountain lion skull and a pocketful of agates and arrowheads. Watch out for the Mexican Trogon—a very pretty bird that yelps like a hen turkey.

If you have any curiosity about nature, carry field guides for birds, mammals, cacti, and trees, especially. Also take a map so you will know where you are. Have your outfitter mark it for you. Photo film may be hard to find, so carry plenty.

What the western subspecies have in common

Although Gould's and Merriam's turkeys do not occur in the same range, they occupy some pretty rugged country and exhibit some of the same habits in feeding, roosting, and traveling. Hunters familiar with hunting both tell me that hunting them is much the same.

Both Gould's and Merriam's, as well as the Rio Grande, gobble in shorter bursts than Eastern or Florida turkeys. They sound like they are saying "gobble, gobble, gobble"—much like domestic turkeys gobbling. The alarm putt of the three western subspecies sounds like "pitt" rather than "putt," and is not as loud as normally rendered by the Eastern and Florida subspecies. The other calls I have heard from the western subspecies are similar to those of the eastern turkeys and, as far as I can tell, the voice differences do not affect hunting technique.

Like the Merriam's and Rio Grande, a Gould's turkey will move as far as it has to, which can be a very long way in the foothills and mountains of Mexico. The Gould's has the same kind of seasonal migration up and down the mountains as the Merriam's, and like the Merriam's, I am told that the Gould's may be absent one year from a range where it was plentiful the year before. Its movement behavior has been little studied, but my experience in the Sierra Madres of Chihuahua suggests that Gould's is a very mobile subspecies. It can be hard to head one off when he starts moving.

Gould's will fly from one mountain ridge to another, passing well out of shotgun range overhead. I photographed a mixed spring mating flock as it flew from a mountain down to the creek valley to feed and water on several afternoons in early May. Each time, before the first bird took wing, it yelped loudly, then one at a time the flock took wing and floated down, covering about one-quarter of a mile in a matter of seconds! Each time, the adult gobblers joined the hens at the bottom by walking down.

The three western subspecies seem to move more than Easterns or Floridas. I have heard the gobbling of Gould's turkeys get about one-eighth of a mile further away with each gobble. This continued until they passed out of hearing distance, which didn't take long. There is a reason for such movement. When roosts are two miles from feeding places, turkeys have to move the two miles, and when summer range is ten miles from winter range, they move between them with little regard for the distance.

One feature of dry climates, especially in Rio Grande and Gould's range, is the cactus and other plants with fleshy stalks and leaves armed with thorns and spines. The water storage requirements of these plants call for the protection of thorns to avoid their being eaten into oblivion during droughts by thirsty animals. So watch where you walk and sit, and what you touch, when you hunt turkeys in the dry Southwest.

Plumage Color Mutants

Above: Speckled gobbler from Florida
(photo David Austin)

Left: Marbled reddish gobbler
(photo Mike McAnany)

Red and white gobbler (photo Jerry Davis)

Above: **Top to bottom, a smoke gray, a normal, a smoke gray, and an erythristic hen**

Left: **Smoke gray hen mount** (courtesy Tony's Taxidermy)

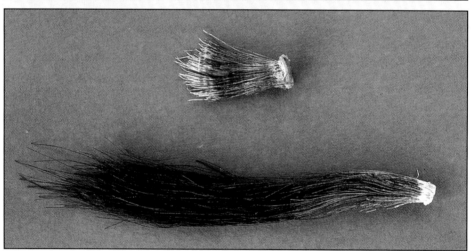

Top: Hen in gobbler plumage, 1995 NWTF Grand Nationals Taxidermy contest. Taxidermy by Bob Skiles.

Above: A normal beard and one that is lacking melanin and is badly abraded from wear

Normal Color Features

Above: **Head colors of adult gobbler in fall**

Left: **Head colors of strutting adult gobbler in spring**

Top: Head colors of a fall jake

Above: Head colors of an adult hen, the year-round. Juvenal hen head colors are similar.

Top left: Amber beard tip of a 1-1/2-year-old gobbler (fall)

Top right: Amber beard tip of a 2-year-old gobbler (spring)

*Above: Spring jake and adult hen showing normal head colors. Hen
is dull grayish; jake is reddish.*

Above: Ocellated turkey gobbler
(photo Curtis Taylor)

Left: Normal leg colors of adult (red) and juvenal (brown) gobblers

The Subspecies
MERRIAM'S

Top: Tail of a Merriam's gobbler

Above: Spring flock of Merriam's
(photo Donald Jones)

Right: Merriam's gobbler in strut
(photo Donald Jones)

The Subspecies
FLORIDA

Top: Tail of a Florida gobbler

Above: Florida gobbler in full strut

Top: Eight osceola hunters; nine gobblers. Who said osceolas were hard?

Above: Small mating flock of Florida wild turkeys

The Subspecies
EASTERN

Top: Tail of an Eastern gobbler

Above: Eastern gobbler in full strut
(photo Glenn Smith)

Top: One gobbler and six hunters in West Virginia. Who said Easterns were easy?

Above: Eastern adult hen

(photo Glenn Smith)

The Subspecies
GOULD'S

Top: Tail of a Gould's gobbler

Above: Spring flock of Gould's turkeys in Mexico

Right: Gould's gobbler in full strut

Top: A well-photographed Gould's turkey in Chihuahua

Above: Typical black toes of adult Gould's gobbler

Left: Camping in Mexico called for skinning our Gould's trophies

The Subspecies
RIO GRANDE

Top: Tail of a Rio Grande gobbler

Left: Rio Grande gobblers in strut
(photo Joe Herrera)

Below: After a successful Rio Grande hunt in Texas

4

Preserving Trophy Parts

A wild turkey's legs, spurs, beard, and plumage are decorative when properly preserved and require minimal space for displaying. Spread tails and wings look good on a den wall and small parts such as spurs and beards can be preserved and put away for safekeeping in display boxes or displayed in shadow boxes. But don't hide your trophies—it is easy to make them worthy additions to your home or lodge decor.

You can use materials available in regular stores and local craft supply shops. If you are seriously interested in doing taxidermy, information and supply sources are available in taxidermy magazines such as *Breakthrough,* P. O. Box 2945, Hammond, LA 70404-2945. A large vendor of taxidermy supplies is Van Dyke's, P. O. Box 278, Woonsocket, SD 57385. Books on taxidermy are available—look in large bookstores or libraries or order them from taxidermy supply houses.

Many of my readers are old classmates of mine at the Northwestern School of Taxidermy in Omaha, Nebraska. We took lessons via mail. Those were the days. Every living thing in four counties around me was endangered, but most of the species have recovered nicely since I slacked up many years ago.

One reason I didn't go into professional taxidermy is because of the preacher's cat. The dearly beloved long-haired gray-colored family pet died in the garage one weekend. The preacher's daughter, about my age in high school, asked me to mount it. I couldn't resist. If you are interested in taxidermy, don't ever skin a cat found dead.

Taxidermy has come a long way since the Northwestern School of Taxidermy, but the old-fashioned ways still work for the things we will be discussing in this chapter.

First, a few basic procedures that apply to all body parts to be saved. All flesh should be removed. Tiny bits that are impossible to remove must be coated with borax or dry taxidermist's preservative while the part is still moist. As the body part dries, keep raw parts coated with the powder and you won't have a problem with it rotting, but do not let the use of borax be an excuse for not properly cleaning the parts of flesh.

Formaldehyde or other liquid preservative should be injected into parts from which you can't remove the flesh, such as the lower legs and feet and the very tip of the wing. If you don't inject the legs, they will eventually attract tiny beetles and other vermin that will make them unsightly.

Formaldehyde has become difficult to buy in recent years. If you know an undertaker, he may be able to help you find embalming fluid. A non-poisonous trade chemical, "Balmex," is available from taxidermy supply houses. You'll need to get a syringe and needle from the taxidermy supply, the pharmacy, or a veterinary supply store. Follow mixing directions for the preservative and inject small amounts into several places in the legs and feet.

Do not use table salt on anything you are preserving at home. Heavy salting will keep flesh and skin from rotting, but will attract moisture every time the atmospheric humidity goes up and that will eventually ruin the specimen.

There are two exceptions to the "no salt" rule. You can pack raw bones in salt and store them unrefrigerated for later use in making wingbones. Remove the salt from the bones when you use them by washing them in water. The other exception is when you have a skin that will have to be washed by the taxidermist anyway. Check in advance to find out whether your taxidermist routinely washes turkey skins. If so, he or she will probably suggest salt instead of borax. But ask first. If in doubt, don't use salt.

Table 4.1. Supplies for preparing wild turkey specimens

Item	Purpose/Comment
Needed in the woods	
Paper towels	Stuff in throat and anus
Towelettes	Clean your hands after gutting
Turkey tote bag	Transport specimen in woods
Needed back at camp	
Cord	If specimen is to hang
Sharp knife	Make it very sharp
*Cornmeal or hardwood sawdust	Absorb body fluids
*Borax or powdered preservative	Preserve skin
*Newspaper or wrapping paper	Wrap finished whole specimen
*Wrapping tape	Tape specimen in paper and in box
*Heavy plastic bags and closure ties	Hold finished specimen
Game shears	Cut difficult body parts
Dish detergent and water	Wash any bloody plumage
Hair blower	Dry any washed plumage
Needed before shipping	
*Cardboard, large piece	Splint the carcass securely
Large corrugated cardboard box	Pack whole specimen to ship
*Portable ice chest	Be sure it's long enough
Other	
*Ice or freezer	Have plenty
Label with address, etc.	For ID and shipping address
Needed at home or in shop	
*Formaldehyde or embalming fluid	Inject feet and legs
*Syringe and needle	Inject embalming fluid
Pins	Hold toes and feathers to dry
*Mounting plaques	For finished tail, feet, etc.
Drying board	Hold parts while drying
*Felt border	Edge tail or other parts

* There are substitutes for many items, some of which will always be available in a hunting camp, but those with this symbol need to be contemplated ahead of time.

If you live in an arid climate, borax-treated turkey skin and other parts will dry almost anywhere you leave them, but keep them out of reach of family pets and wild varmints before, during, and after drying. If you live where the climate is humid, dry your trophies in an air-conditioned or dehumidified environment.

If oil is noticeable on any turkey part you are preserving, clean it with a solvent such as mineral spirits, acetone, or unleaded gasoline. If the feathers are only slightly soiled, you can dab them with a soapy wet cloth and dry them with cornmeal or hardwood sawdust. If the feather vane separates when you are cleaning the feather, gently groom the feather back after it dries. Separated feather parts are designed by nature to stick back together. Birds keep their feathers tidy by frequent preening, which you can emulate with your fingers.

If your specimen's feathers get wet, dry them by dusting repeatedly with hardwood sawdust or cornmeal to soak up the moisture. Apply fresh, dry cornmeal until they are dry and fluff them with an electric hair blower. If you are in the woods, you can do the job without the hair blower; it will just take more applications of cornmeal, and more time.

Don't use a hairbrush on the plumage. Brushing will separate the vane of the feathers in a way that cannot easily be made whole again.

Decide ahead of time what you want to do with your turkey trophy parts and review this chapter so that you will have what you need for the job (Table 4.1).

Preserving Beards

If you jerk off the beard, it will eventually fall apart. It is best to cut it off, leaving a small piece of skin at its base (Fig. 4.1) to hold the bristles together and to provide substance for gluing or tacking on a display board or plaque. Dab dry preservative on the raw end while it is still moist enough for the powder to stick. That's all there is to preserving the beard.

Preserving Legs and Spurs

One way to save the leg spurs is to cut off the whole unfeathered lower legs (Fig. 4.2), inject a few drops of a liquid preservative or formaldehyde into the feet and soft parts (Fig. 4.3), and let them dry whole.

Fig. 4.1. *Beard removed with skin left at the base*

Arrange the toes the way you want them before they stiffen by pinning them on a piece of plastic foam, soft wood, or cardboard. Hat pins, plain straight pins, or small nails are okay. Place the pins or nails beside the toes to hold them in place. Use twine to hold the leg upright in place (Fig. 4.4).

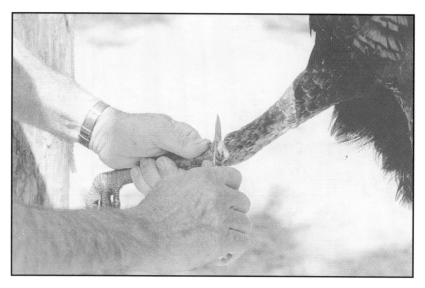

Fig. 4.2. *The lower leg being cut off at the joint*

You sometimes see dried turkey legs that appear silvered on the surface. That is caused by the separation of the leg scales from the underlying tissue and is most likely to happen when the legs were cured in a warm environment. It is best to freeze-dry the injected lower legs by placing them in the freezer, uncovered, or allow the legs to dry in a cool, dehumidified environment—an air-conditioned room is usually satisfactory.

Fig. 4.3. *Foot being injected with formaldehyde to embalm it*

Fig. 4.4. *Foot drying in standing position*

When the legs are dry, paint them with clear shellac or similar covering and spray the end joint with a persistent roach poison. Non-glossy coatings look better than glossy types. It is best not to try to color the legs. It will be very difficult for you to match the color. The natural color will usually be present if the legs are dried properly.

Fig. 4.6. *Dried feet on display, cut off below the main joint*

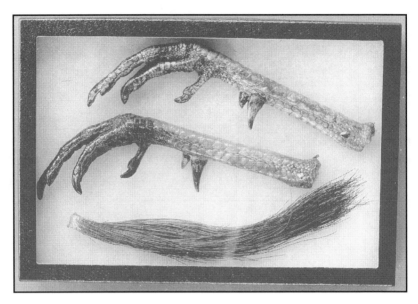

Fig. 4.5. Beard and legs displayed in a glass-fronted box

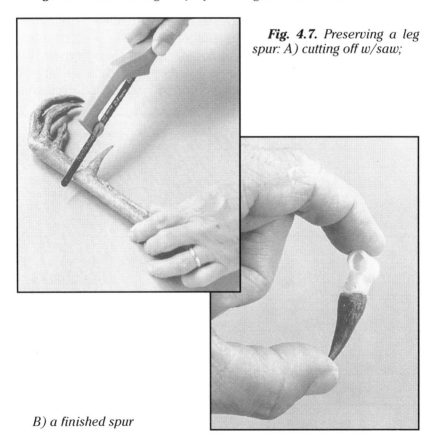

Fig. 4.7. Preserving a leg spur: A) cutting off w/saw;

B) a finished spur

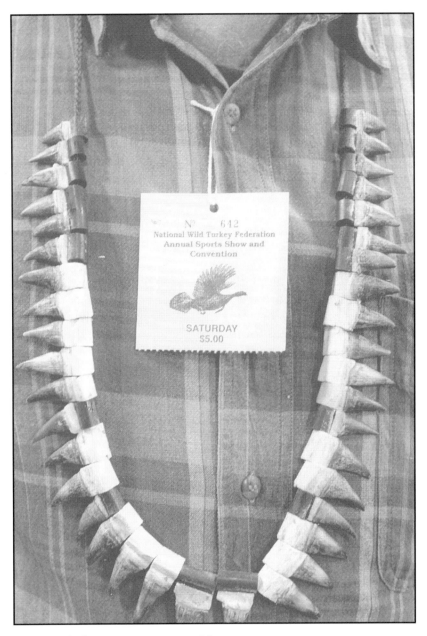

Fig. 4.8. Spurs strung as a necklace

Some hunters like to cut off and keep only a short piece of the leg with the spur on it. For this, cut completely across the bone on both sides close to the spur (Fig. 4.7A). Remove the skin from the bone around the spur and clean out the hollow bone (Fig. 4.7B). You can leave the leg scales on if you wish.

Preserving Wings and Tails

The wings and tail reveal the main color differences among the wild turkey subspecies, which makes them especially good wall trophies for your grand slam. Even if you are not into grand slamming, a turkey tail or wing makes an attractive wall mount for the den or trophy room.

Wings

Cut the wing off close to the breast (Fig. 4.9) leaving some of the shoulder plumage attached. You can remove any excess shoulder skin later.

Cut the skin open along the underside of the wing. Since you will display only the back of the wing, don't be concerned about the condition of the skin on the underside. You can remove the wing bones for making yelpers or leave them in the wing.

Fig. 4.9. *Cutting off a wing to preserve separately (Photo Sandra Prescott)*

Fig. 4.10. *Wing with books to hold it in position as it dries*

There are three wing sections: a meaty segment at the shoulder associated with the humerus bone; a section in the middle wing associated with the ulna and radius bones; and a smaller segment at the wing tip. You will have to dig around to get all the flesh from between and under the wing bones. Be careful not to cut off the bases of the feathers that project into the skin. Inject the wing section at the tip with liquid preservative and apply borax to the raw parts.

When all the flesh has been removed and dry preservative applied, spread the wing the way you want it to dry and place objects such as books on the large feathers to hold the wing in position as it stiffens (Fig. 4.10). When you place the weights, permit the incision to be exposed to hasten drying.

In a day or two, the feathers will begin to stiffen in place. Check their rigidity while adjustments can still be made. After a few more days, the dried feathers will be permanently set.

If you removed the bones for making yelpers, replace the bones with something rigid to support the open wing. Stiff cardboard or a piece of thin wood can be sewed or glued to the skin from the underside to replace the bones. Do that after the wing dries.

*Fig. **4.11.** Removing the tail: A) begin cut high on the back;*

B) cut tail off carcass after skinning down the back;

C) tail should have ample back plumage attached (Photos Sandra Prescott)

Tail

If you want to save the tail, be especially careful to protect the tips of the feathers. Guard against the outer margin being forced backwards against anything as you transport it in the woods and when you get it in the truck or at home.

To remove the tail, hang the specimen by the neck as you would for skinning as described in Chapter 8, cut the skin across the middle of the back, and peel the skin from the body toward the tail. Expose the base of the tail and cut the tail off the carcass where it narrows down just before the "pope's nose" (Fig. 4.11). Be sure to leave some of the back skin with the tail. If you don't take enough back feathers, there will be an unappealing featherless zone at the base of the tail.

The tail bone terminates in a V-shaped configuration where the large feathers are inserted—like an oversized chicken tail. Remove that bone, along with the associated muscle and fat (Fig. 4.12). The tail will be displayed in a position that will hide the underside, so don't be concerned about how the base looks on that side.

Before beginning your cut to remove the tail bone, wiggle some of the tail feathers to see how they are inserted into the base so you'll know where to cut. Cut out the bone. If you cut deeply into the V, some of the large feathers may come out. Work slowly and carefully and that won't happen.

With the tail bone out, you will be able to remove most of the remaining flesh and fat. Blot and rub the fat with a cloth rag or paper towel and keep picking at it with a knife. Any fat left will gradually liquefy and flow onto the feathers in a few months. Removing the fat from the base of the tail requires fifteen to twenty minutes for a thorough job.

When all the fat and flesh have been removed, put another application of borax on the raw parts. Lay the tail in a safe place with a cup of cornmeal piled on the moist base where the fat was removed and leave it overnight at room temperature. The cornmeal will absorb some of the fat. If the cornmeal becomes heavily stained with oil overnight, repeat the process with a fresh pile. Hardwood sawdust can be used in place of cornmeal.

After cleaning up the fat, place the tail flat on a large piece of wood, cardboard, plastic foam, or something similar. Spread the feathers the way you want them to dry and place books or other weights on the tail as you would on the wing. You can pin some of the feathers to hold them the way you want them to dry (Fig. 4.13). Put the tail in a safe place to dry.

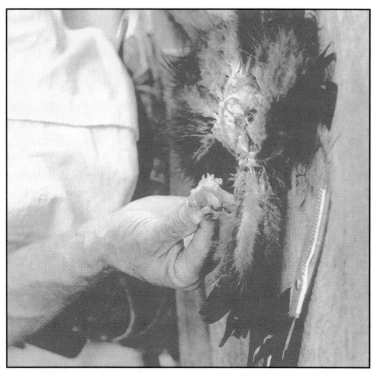

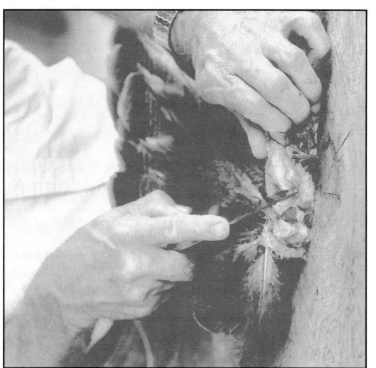

B) the tail bone and associated muscle and fat in hand (Photos Sandra Prescott)

Fig. 4.12. *Cutting bone out of removed tail: A) cutting out the "V" with knife;*

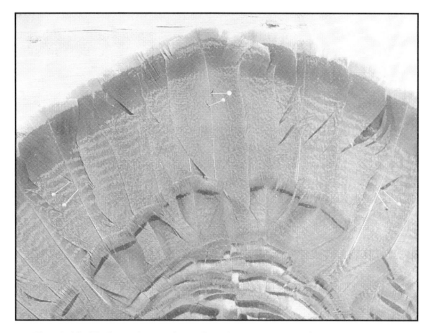

Fig. 4.13. Tail on drying board with pins to hold feathers in place

What was said about drying the wing applies also to the tail—check it every day or two as it dries so you can be sure it ends up spread the way you want it. It is usually attractive to mount all your turkey tails so that they are spread similarly.

When the tail is stiff, take a knife, toenail clippers, or small scissors and remove any remaining dried meat and fat from the base where you took out the bone. It is easier to remove some of the last small bits after they are dry.

It is a good idea to stuff a small wad of paper toweling or cloth rag into the void where you removed the "pope's nose." The towel will absorb some of the oil that oozes out over time. After a few months, remove the towel and replace it with clean cloth or paper towel if it is stained with oil.

Trim the excess back skin, but be aware that the feathers of the rump have their roots well up on the back. Do any trimming a little at a time.

The very bottom end of the tail will reveal the unattractive feather bases and needs to be covered. A small plaque is good for that. You may also use cloth or leather, a simple piece of thin wood, or a patch of short plumage from some other part of the bird. If you use a piece of wood, cover it with cloth or leather, or paint it.

If you remove and save all of the back plumage with the tail mount, the result is called a "cape." Just begin your skinning at the upper neck instead of the mid-back and leave the skin attached to the tail.

Wall Rug and Shoulder Mount

A shoulder mount with the head on is a job for a taxidermist, but you can make an attractive wall rug yourself without the head.

For a wall rug, you will display the whole skin flat (Fig. 4.14) instead of making it look like a live turkey. Use of the legs is optional.

Fig. 4.14. *Wall rug mounted directly on wall*

Fig. 4.15. *Tail and beard mounted with store-bought display kit*

Skinning is similar to that for whole body mounting, discussed in Chapter 5, except that you cut open the entire underside of the bird from the neck to the anus rather than placing only one hole in the belly. Hold the borax until the skinning is done if you want to eat the flesh.

Remove all flesh and fat and cover the raw side with borax. Place the skin flat on a large piece of cardboard, plywood, or plastic foam exactly as you want it to dry. Carefully pin it with the raw side out—open it completely, but do not overstretch the hide.

If you want to use the head on the flat skin, check with your taxidermist about preserving the head. If you leave the legs on the skin, they should be injected and fixed firmly to the mounting board or to the wall.

Ways to Display Body Parts

Suitable mounting materials are available from building materials stores and craft supply shops. Glass front display boxes are available from knife dealer catalogs and trophy shops. Beards and/or legs look good in glass display boxes or shadow boxes and, if properly preserved, will keep nicely that way.

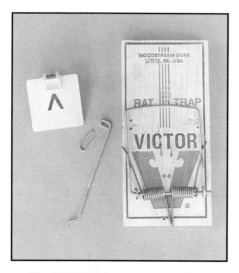

Fig. 4.16. Making a rat trap tail mount:
A) unneeded parts removed and the
spring relocated to bottom of base;

For maximum protection and durability, beards can be imbedded in epoxy resin and used as paperweights. Check at large flea markets for people selling epoxy-covered items, such as pictures on wood, to find a craftsman to mount your beards and spurs in epoxy, or buy what you need at a craft supply store to do it yourself.

Brackets for beard displays are available from hunting supply dealers and taxidermists. Some are designed for displaying several beards and some are for both beards and a tail. If you plan to use a kit, buy one ahead of time and follow the instructions that come with it.

A tail can be displayed on an easel or some similar propping device.

B) dried tail inserted;

One way to mount a tail on the wall is to use a large rat trap with the spring parts rearranged. The trap springs will hold the tail in place against the trap base. The wooden base will be the mounting platform.

Discard the bait treadle and the wire that holds the trap when set. Remove the staples from the metal parts, move the springs to the bottom of the wooden platform, and replace the staples there. Use epoxy glue or small staples to affix a thin board to the outside of the trap's wire hoop. Paint or cover the board

C) back view to show trap base board;

D) finished job with a leather-covered board glued or stapled to front of trap wire

as you would a plaque. Open the spring and stick the tail into the trap, allowing the force of the spring to hold the tail in place. Place a small staple on the top of the trap and hang it on the wall. You can have a metal or plastic plate engraved by the trophy shop with the date of the kill and other data.

The purpose of the thin board on the rat trap, or the wooden plaque in the store-bought kits, is to cover the unfeathered base of the turkey tail and to provide a place for a hook and for an inscription or other pertinent information.

There are many ways to cover the base of the tail and mount it on the wall. You can sew leather or felt directly to the tail base and, with a loop of twine, hang the tail upside down—or whatever you choose.

A wall rug can be mounted on a precut piece of thin plywood or similar flat base with glue and carpet tacks and then hung on the wall. Or, you can tack the skin directly to the wall with small brads. A cape can be mounted as would a wall rug.

Whole skins are attractive in a trophy room when hung by the legs like birds recently shot. You can hang the skin without the head or use an artificial one. Follow the skinning instructions for whole body mounting in the next chapter. Hang the skin while it is still limp and sew it up with thread to close any large openings. Two turkey skins look good together.

Fig. 4.17. Tail, wings, legs, and beard mounted on a board for display on an artist's easel (Courtesy Florida Chapter NWTF)

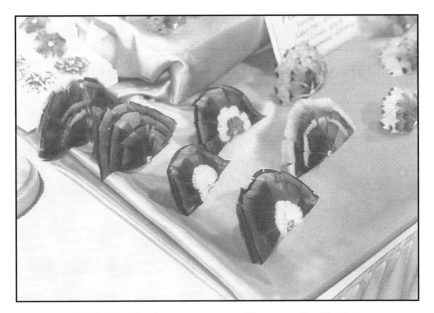

Fig. 4.18. Turkey feather ornaments (Courtesy Pat Tuttle)

Wings can be hung on the wall. Before the wing completely dries, tie a small wire loop to a bone on the underside and hang the wing as you would a picture. Pick the balance point for the wire so it will hang level.

You can use pliers or wire cutters to modify a small spring wire plate hanger to grasp the wing by the bones on the underside. Then hang it like a plate on the wall.

Spurs can be strung together and worn as a necklace or a hat band, or used on a key chain or some other ornament. Some jewelers will make your spurs into gold-plated pendants or lapel pins.

Dried legs can be saved in any position in which they dry or the toes can be spread as described earlier and the feet mounted on a board or plaque. If dried with the toes spread as though walking, a leg will stand alone on your desk or table and will look good there mounted on a thin plaque.

I have seen advertisements for bronzing turkey legs as you might do baby shoes. Watch the turkey magazines for ads, or check with a taxidermist or someone that bronzes baby shoes.

If you do woodworking, leathercraft, or sewing, you can make your own display accessories. Look through hunting supply catalogs for display ideas and make your own.

5

A Specimen for the Taxidermist

If you plan to have a taxidermist work on your trophy, discuss it with one beforehand. He can offer information about care and preparation of the specimen and tell you how to get it to him. Taxidermists do shoulder mounts, wall rugs, and whole turkeys. Whole turkeys in strutting and flying postures usually cost more than standing. Expect to pay from $300-$500 for a whole-bird mount.

Don't allow an amateur to mount your trophy unless you plan to let him keep it. Amateurs who do acceptable jobs on deer heads will fall short on your wild turkey trophy. Birds are especially difficult for many amateurs. I have never seen a satisfactory turkey mounting job by a non-professional. Select a commercial taxidermist based on work you know was done by him. Look at his turkey work and be sure that the same person in the shop will be doing your bird.

Looking at competition mounts is one way to judge taxidermy, but be aware that the job you get will not match the work done by the same taxidermist for competitive purposes. Contest work is done with the judges in mind and is very time consuming. Judges have esoteric ways to grade the work and taxidermists have to do contest work with that in mind.

Discuss with your taxidermist the mount's posture and substrate and the type of head and neck you want. The head types to choose from are freeze-dried, head skin from the dead bird, artificial material molded from the dead bird, or preformed of plastic.

Taking Care of the Specimen

If you don't get complete instructions on field care from a taxidermist, here is what to do.

Be sure to have in camp a large plastic bag and a cooler large enough to hold the bird without jamming the tail. You will need ice or a refrigerator if you plan to take the whole specimen to the taxidermist intact, and a box of salt or borax if you plan to do any skinning. Table 4.1 lists the supplies you will need. Look over the list and see how much applies to your plans. Read through this chapter for ideas of other things to have on hand.

Take with you to the woods a couple of paper towels. Shoot the gobbler in the head and hope that he dies calmly. As you have seen before, he will probably do some flouncing as he expires.

Do not try to restrain a turkey as it dies unless you have experience handling live turkeys. Don't pick up the bird by the legs—you can get a nasty spur stab. Don't try to hold him down—you'll just knock more feathers out. If you have to handle a dying turkey for some compelling reason, hold him by one leg in each hand and watch out for the spurs.

Broken wings and legs, plumage flounced in mud and smeared with blood, and shot-up wing and tail feathers will not make a good mounted specimen. Taxidermists can wash specimens, but washed bird plumage usually does not look as good as plumage that did not require washing. I have mounted birds myself and I know that a clean skin makes a better mount.

If a turkey is disabled but has its eyes wide open, approach ready to shoot again. Stand far enough away so that a second shot will not ruin the specimen and, if you do have to shoot, be careful to shoot him in the head. A taxidermist can fix up a badly shot head better than a shot up carcass.

If the turkey does not die within a few minutes, finish him off with a blow to the back of the head with the nearest thing to a blackjack you can find. When the turkey stops moving, handle it by its bare legs or neck. Place no stress on the body feathers— they will come out easily while the specimen is warm. Poke one

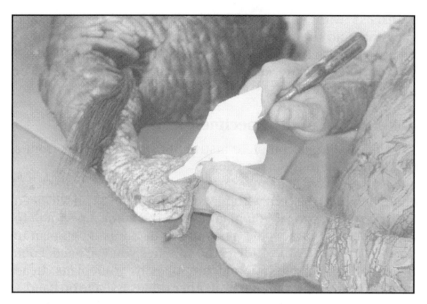

Fig. 5.1. *Stuff paper towel into the throat to absorb excess moisture. Do the same with the anus.*

or two paper towels into the throat to block and absorb blood and mucous that might otherwise ooze out. Turn the specimen carefully and look for large spots of blood and pick off any you find. Avoid blotting globs of blood with tissue—that usually spreads it.

Check the gobbler's anus. If a formed dropping is on the way out, help it out. If there is excessive moisture at the anus, wipe it and poke a paper towel or toilet tissue two or three inches into the anus using a small stick.

Taxidermists can glue back in a few dislodged feathers, so save any large feathers that come out. If a large patch of small feathers is pulled out, save what you can of them but don't be concerned about only a dozen or so lost body feathers.

If you cannot get the specimen into a freezer within about two hours, remove the entrails in the field to hasten cooling. Make a small lengthwise incision below the breast. Don't extend the incision longer than required to get your hand inside.

Reach inside and get a handful of guts, and pull them out. Be careful not to get blood on the plumage when you are gutting the bird. You'll need to cut the intestine off at the anus. Prop open the body cavity with a small stick and let it cool to air temperature. Even late spring air is cooler than the 102° turkey body temperature.

Clean your hands with towelettes, which you should carry in your pocket. (They are on the list.) Don't get blood or other body fluids on your gun—they are salty and will cause rust.

It is best not to try to eat the specimen if you plan a whole body mount, but if you must remove the breast meat, open the skin along the midline of the breast just enough to remove the muscle with a long-bladed knife. Simply enlarge the cut in the skin you made when you gutted the bird. Cut the breast muscle out in pieces—it'll need to be cut up anyway for frying.

A tote bag is useful in getting the specimen out of the woods in good condition. Let the carcass cool a few minutes and allow the feathers to set more firmly before placing it in the tote bag. Smooth the feathers into their natural positions and wrap the carcass neatly in the bag, being careful not to crumple the feathers. Haul it head first so as not to damage the tail feathers on vegetation.

Keep the specimen in the shade and away from sources of heat and flies. Do not place it in a plastic bag until it goes into refrigeration. A warm specimen will spoil quickly in a bag. If the specimen spoils, some of the feathers will come out and the taxidermist cannot save it.

If the specimen is to hang for more than two or three hours, do not hang it by the legs. That will cause body fluids to flow to the head and swell it grotesquely. Lay the specimen flat or hang it by the head.

Fig. 5.2. *Swollen head of gobbler left hanging by its legs*

To ready the specimen for the cooler, lay it out and wrap the head and neck in paper towels, tissue, or a cloth rag. Tuck the head under a wing. Press the wings to the body and wrap the whole body in a double layer of newspaper, like a mummy. Tape the paper in place on the body but leave the tail feathers sticking out.

Place the wrapped carcass on a piece of stiff cardboard that protrudes beyond the tail. The cardboard beyond the tail is to prevent the tail from touching the container. Tape the wrapped specimen to the cardboard like a body splint so that it cannot shift in transport. Be especially careful about cramping the tail. Stuff paper and other soft material into the cooler with the carcass to keep it from shifting in transit. Mark the top of the container "THIS SIDE UP."

It is much easier to get the bird in a cooler while it is still pliable, but it becomes very difficult to pack one after it is frozen. It is best to freeze the specimen in a portable cooler with the lid open. If you have to freeze the whole specimen before placing it in a portable cooler, be sure to freeze the carcass in a compact posture that will fit into the cooler after it stiffens.

If you are not freezing the bird, prepare the carcass as for freezing and refrigerate it with ice. Leave the ice in plastic bags without leaks. Double bagging is a good idea. If possible, stick a half-gallon plastic milk carton of frozen water into the body cavity. If you have "blue ice" bags, they are good. Use two plastic garbage bags or a thick cadaver bag for the carcass. If you know a coroner, ask him or her about a cadaver bag. Your taxidermist may have a suitable bag as well.

Deliver the specimen to a taxidermist on ice or in frozen condition. A hard frozen specimen in an insulated cooler will keep in shipment for three or four days. Even in a plain corrugated cardboard box, a frozen turkey will normally be in good shape after a two-day trip. If it thaws, refreeze it at the first opportunity. If you can't freeze it, keep it cold.

You won't be mounting every turkey you shoot and there will always be another. My suggestion is to be prepared to not mount any specimen that is in questionable condition. Wait for a perfect example of the beautiful wild turkey. If it's not in good shape, take a lot of pictures, save the beard and spurs, and eat it.

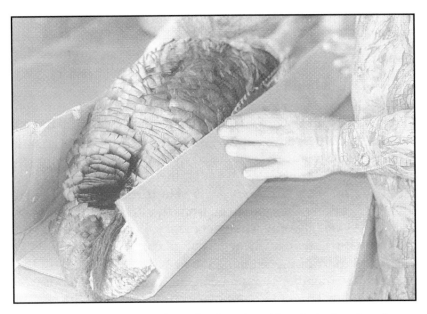

Fig. 5.3. *Preparing specimen for freezing: A) tuck the head and wrap the wings to the body; B) tape the carcass tightly in cardboard with the cardboard extending beyond the end of the tail*

Skinning a Turkey

As already advised, it is best to get the whole carcass to the taxidermist—don't skin it unless you are a taxidermist yourself or there is some compelling reason to do so.

If you know in advance that you will skin the specimen, you should read and take with you a how-to book on taxidermy. If you are really serious about this, practice in advance by skinning a bird you don't plan to mount. Use a pheasant or grouse if you don't have an extra turkey.

I will stress these things: Find out from your taxidermist whether to use borax or table salt on the skin. If your taxidermist routinely washes all turkey skins, he may say to use salt, but many taxidermists prefer borax. Also, ask him how he wants you to deal with the head—some say cut it off, some say leave it on, some say to skin it.

When you skin a specimen for taxidermy, the idea is to remove the skin without cutting any more holes in it than necessary. Ideally, you should make only one hole. If there is a dead turkey in camp that is not to be mounted, practice on it first to see what you are up against. Scan the rest of this chapter before you begin.

Begin by placing the specimen on a large piece of wrapping paper or newspapers spread out on a large table or other work surface. Have everything on hand for the job. Be careful about the tip of the tail. Do not let it stick off the edge of the table where you will press against it as you work.

With the bird on its back, make an incision barely through the skin of the lower breast, beginning about where the breast bone ends at the belly. Cut just through the skin down to and through the top side of the anus. Avoid cutting deeply enough to expose the entrails—just through the skin.

Get the turkey's body out of its skin through the hole you made by working the skin away from the body wall with your fingers. Use a knife only when necessary. Be careful pulling on the skin—it will tear easily in certain places.

The first part of the skinning job is awkward because of the tight skin. Remember that you can cut any part of the body or bones you need to, but do not make another hole in the skin.

With your fingers, work the skin away from the body in the direction of the thighs and ribs. When you can see the "knee" joint, sever the leg at the joint. That will be a little awkward because of the tight working room. With the joint severed, you have the room needed to skin out the "drumstick." Do the same with the other leg. The thighs will be left attached to the body. Cut the meat off the drumstick bones and leave the bones on the skin.

With legs cut loose from the thighs, it will be easy to work the skin away from the thighs, which will provide more slack skin to work the skin loose toward and around the anus.

Getting the tail off can be tricky if you are not familiar with bird anatomy, but anybody can do it. Cut through the belly and intestine at the anus, all the way to the back, to expose a spot of the backbone. Any spot will do. When you can see the bone, cut through the bone at a joint. Any joint will do.

At this stage, I recommend turning the carcass on its head with the breast down and tail in the air so you can finish severing the tail from the carcass. Do not cut the skin. When you have cut across the flesh holding the tail to the carcass, the tail will flop down over the back and you will have a good picture of where you are headed. Start working the skin away from the carcass up the back. Leave the cut-off tail bone (the "pope's nose") in the tail for now.

With the carcass standing on its head, work the skin over the back in the direction of the wings. When you get to the base of the wing, cut one wing off at its junction with the body. That will give you more working room.

Pull the first bone of the wing out of the skin, as you did the drum bone, and cut the muscle off the largest wing bone. Leave the rest of the wing bones attached to each other. Repeat the process with the other wing. (Later you will cut open the middle section of the wing from the underside to remove the meat.)

You should have discussed with your taxidermist how to remove the head. Follow his instructions. I usually leave the skull attached but unskinned by cutting the neck off inside the skin. Some taxidermists recommend cutting the head completely off where the bare skin joins the neck feathers. The head can be difficult to skin if it is left on without making another cut in the throat or back of the head.

With the skin and head off the carcass, cut the bone out of the tail and remove the flesh from the middle section of the wing by making an incision along the underside. Both of these processes are described in Chapter 4. Don't try to flesh out the tip of the wing—just the two sections where the most meat is. Don't inject anything into the body parts if it is going to the taxidermist.

Go over the skin and rub, pull, tear, and cut off any remaining pieces of flesh. Now comes the question of using salt versus borax. Get that clarified by your taxidermist ahead of time. If in doubt, use borax or dry preservative.

After salting or boraxing, lay the skin so that the feathers are not seriously wrinkled, in the shade. Do not try to dry out the skin. Place paper towels next to the raw skin and roll the skin up loosely so that the raw side is inside, against the paper. Place the rolled skin in an airtight plastic bag and freeze it or keep it refrigerated. Do not allow the skin to get any wetter, any dryer, or to freezer burn.

Before you leave the specimen with your taxidermist, be sure he understands how you want the mounted bird positioned and the type of head you want. Look at examples of head types and discuss this with him. It is a good idea to state your preferences in writing so as not to rely too much on his or his assistant's memory.

Transporting and Shipping

Check with your airline company about how best to ship your specimen to the taxidermist. Most will accept plastic coolers containing frozen carcasses. Airlines do not permit shipment with dry ice because of the pressure the CO_2 creates as it evaporates—an airtight container might explode in the baggage compartment.

You may be able to check the cooler as you would luggage and take it to the taxidermist yourself.

Getting a Specimen Out of Mexico

You may have trouble getting your Gould's or Rio Grande specimen out of Mexico because of regulations of the U. S. Department of Agriculture. The law is in the Code of Federal Regulations, Title 9, Part 94.6. The importation regulations apply to all wildlife specimens. Your hunting outfitter should be able to advise you about this. If you don't know what to do, you could lose your Gould's specimen at the border.

The problem is a U. S. government-perceived possibility that certain poultry diseases will be imported into the U. S. on dead wild turkeys. The USDA requires that you carry or ship raw skins or body parts directly to a USDA certified taxidermist in the states, by a bonded shipper. A list of approved taxidermists is available from the Administrator, Import-Export Products Staff, VS-APHIS, U. S. Department of Agriculture, Room 757, Federal Building, 6505 Belcrest Road, Hyattsville, MD 20782. Your taxidermist will know whether he is on the list and, if not, he may wish to apply for certification at the same address. Bonded shippers are available for the asking at all border ports.

If the skin has already been treated as a taxidermist normally would, or the specimen has been mounted for display, there are no restrictions about bringing it across the border other than those related to importation of endangered species under the authority of the U. S. Fish and Wildlife Service. Endangered species regulations do not apply to the wild turkey in Mexico. You will need to show your hunting license at the border and the carcass must be tagged in accord with Mexican game laws.

USDA regulations require decontamination of any flesh from your specimen by the approved taxidermist in the U. S. For game birds, all the taxidermist has to do is incinerate or boil any fragments of flesh he removes. He does not have to do anything special to the skin. There is no fumigation process for birds.

You may be able to legally carry a skinned specimen with you overland through border ports of entry. A Veterinary Service form 16-78 has to be issued by a USDA officer at the port of entry. To be on the safe side, you should ask the USDA about the form and any other red tape when you enter Mexico, or have your outfitter check that out for you well in advance.

If you fly out of Mexico, you can ship the specimen by air directly to a certified taxidermist. That should be discussed in advance with your taxidermist and the airline. The law requires that a USDA employee seal the container and that it be shipped by a bonded shipper. Your taxidermist will have to pick up the specimen at the airport. If your taxidermist is certified by the USDA for importation of game from restricted countries, he will know what to do.

The good news is that turkey specimens are often checked through the border without any questions or problems. That is more likely at small ports of entry and on weekends and holidays, so be prepared to consummate the red tape just in case. Don't create any problems yourself by saying anything you are not asked about.

If you have done what you are supposed to do and still get a hassle from the USDA at the port of entry, you should call one of your U. S. senators or congressmen by phone from the port of entry while you are still very angry. Be sure to have their phone numbers with you just in case. If your congressman or senator can't help get your specimen across, you will know how to vote in the next election. Your timely complaint may help the next Gould's hunter or help you next the time you hunt in Mexico.

All of the above sounds complicated and it can be, but your outfitter should be able to handle it for you and to properly advise you. Question him ahead of time about getting your specimen back. If he can't guarantee it, find another outfitter.

If You Are a Taxidermist

If you are into taxidermy as a professional, you may consider entering the National Wild Turkey Federation's taxidermy contest held annually in connection with the annual late winter convention.

The "Grand National" championships are judged by a panel of biologists and hunters. There is an entry fee and awards are given. For a copy of the rules and regulations, contact the NWTF at P. O. Box 530, Edgefield, SC 29824.

Whether you are a taxidermist or not, the Grand Nationals is a good place to see examples of excellent taxidermy work. You can see the body postures that taxidermists do. Take your camera to the Grand Nationals and show your pictures to your taxidermist before you have your trophy mounted. Showing him the pictures will let him know you have high standards.

One of the main errors I have noticed in otherwise good taxidermy work is the head coloring. The head and neck have to be painted after they dry. Taxidermists sometimes put too much or too little white on the top of the head and excessive blue on the side of the face. Sometimes the colors are not confined to the regions of the head where they belong and there is often too much red. There is sometimes far too much dewlap on a strutting gobbler.

If you have a good color photo of your freshly killed turkey's head, give it to your taxidermist. Head coloring changes slowly on a recently killed turkey; sometimes not at all for an hour or two. Take a close-up photo of your gobbler's head if you like the colors. If you have magazine photos that you like, leave them with your taxidermist. The figures on the color pages of this book depict the natural postures and head coloring of turkeys. Take the book to your taxidermist, but don't leave it with him—he'll get blood stains on it. Give him my address so that he can buy a copy of his own.

There may be small differences in head coloring among the subspecies, but I have not noticed anything significant. There is so much variation within the same populations that average differences would be very difficult to detect.

6

The Wingbone Yelper

(Photo by Sandra Prescott)

The Indians killed and ate turkeys and used their wing feathers to fletch arrows, their spurs for arrow points, and their breast feathers to make blankets. They also wore turkey plumage in important ceremonies and made yelpers of the turkeys' wing bones to call up more turkeys. What a system.

European settlers, who had used animal bones in making game calls in the old country, quickly adopted the Indians' wingbone yelper and added other turkey bones, wooden tubes, bamboo stems, and even cow horns to their yelpers to modulate and amplify the sound.

The principle is simple. Skilled wingbone users can imitate turkey calls on common soda straws, fountain pen tubes, smoking pipe stems, or almost any other small hollow tube. But nothing matches a wingbone yelper made from a wild turkey you took yourself.

Your wingbone yelper will be an ally of the hunt that will last more than a lifetime and will be unexcelled in its grace, beauty, tradition and, most importantly, in imitating the voice of the wild turkey. In this chapter I will explain how to make and use wingbone yelpers.

The small bone from the middle wing of a wild turkey is used as a mouthpiece in all true "wingbone" yelpers. It is possible to yelp satisfactorily on any small tube, as just mentioned, but I won't be discussing the imitations. Although other turkey bones and bones of other animals can be used in combination with the small wing bone, I will refer to turkey bone yelpers as "wingbone yelpers" regardless of the other components.

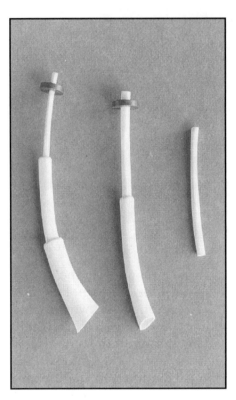

Fig. 6.1. Basic wingbone yelpers: 3-bone, 2-bone, single bone

Yelper Types

The simplest wingbone yelper consists of only the hollow *radius* bone of the turkey's wing (Fig. 6.3). This is what the Indians are said to have used. They also stuck the radius into the *ulna* (Harlan 1994, p. 92) in a manner similar to the classic two-bone yelper I will describe. I do not know whether the Indians made yelpers any more elaborate than that.

Three-bone yelpers can be made with the radius, ulna and either the *humerus* bone of the wing, the thigh bone called the *femur*, or the "drum bone," which is technically called the *tibiotarsus*.

How to Make a Yelper

Good yelpers can be made from the bones of either hens or gobblers or combinations of bones from the two sexes. Pen-reared varieties of wild turkey raised on good diets have satisfactory bones for yelpers, but the bones of most grocery store turkeys are too thin, brittle, and porous. They also have holes that are too large and are often discolored. Normal cooking does not harm the bones.

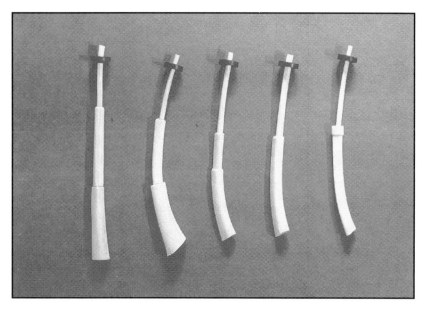

Fig. 6.2. *Five yelper models the author produces, left to right: straight leg, 3-bone with humerus, 3-bone with ulna, 2-bone with ulna, hen ulna and radius with collar*

The bones to use

The radius is needed for the mouthpiece. In humans and other mammals, the radius is the larger of the two middle arm bones, but in turkeys and other birds, the ulna is the larger.

Figure 6.3 shows the location of the yelper bones in the turkey. The humerus is the largest bone of the wing that connects the radius and ulna to the breast—it is the turkey's "shoulder" bone. The femur is the bone of the thigh. The tibiotarsus is the drumstick bone. The tarsometatarsus is the bone of the scaly lower leg that connects to the foot.

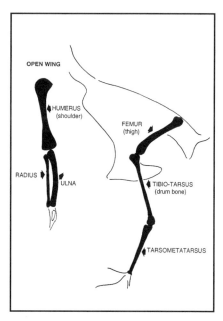

Fig. 6.3. *The turkey bones used for yelpers*

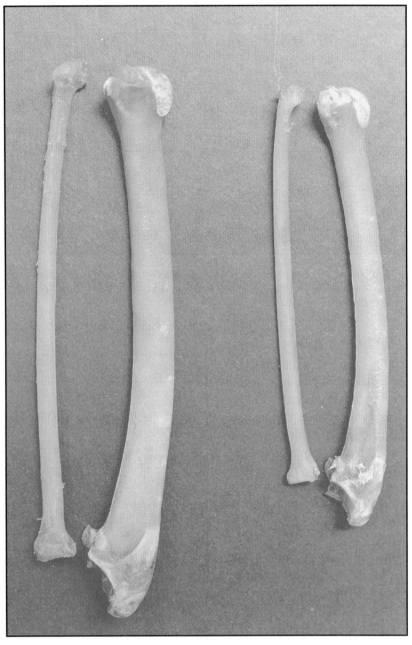

Fig. 6.4. Hen radius and ulna (right) and gobbler radius and ulna

It is sometimes said that a good yelper can be made only with the radius bone of an adult hen as the mouthpiece. Not so. Experienced wingbone users can make any sound with a gobbler radius that they can make with an adult hen radius. Wing bones of small young hens taken in fall may be too small to make good turkey tones. The large radius bones of grown male turkeys tend to produce lower tones than do the smaller bones of hens or fall jakes. The lower-pitched tones are good for jake and gobbler hunting in the fall, while the higher pitch of the hen's voice is more appealing to adult gobblers in spring hunting. The radius bones of fall jakes are satisfactory for making both gobbler and hen tones.

Radius and ulna bones from a hen work well together. Yelpers made of hen bones, being smaller than those with gobbler bones, have a slightly higher pitch and are not as loud, but both pitch and volume are within the natural range of the wild turkey's voice.

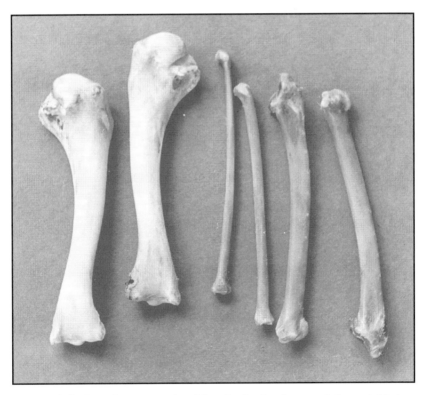

Fig. 6.5. Set of uncut and unbleached wing bones, left to right: two humerus bones, two radii, and two ulnas. The humerii are whiter because they do not contain marrow.

Humerus and femur bones from hens, jakes, or gobblers are okay in combination with any size radius and ulna as long as they can be made to fit together.

The bones of other birds and mammals can be used. I have seen yelpers made with components of deer, Canada goose, vulture, sheep, mountain lion, brown pelican, and sandhill crane bones. It is not legal to shoot non-game species or to use their bones even when you find a specimen already dead.

Museums clean the major flesh from animal bones in a dermestid beetle colony, soak them in ammonium hydroxide, remove the fat with carbon tetrachloride or a dry-cleaning solvent, and bleach the bones in a solution of hydrogen peroxide. If you have access to such chemicals, you probably already know the technique or know somebody who does. If so, take advantage of the opportunity, but most turkey hunters will be do-it-yourselfers and can clean the bones just as well with supplies available at home. Table 6.1 is a list of what you need.

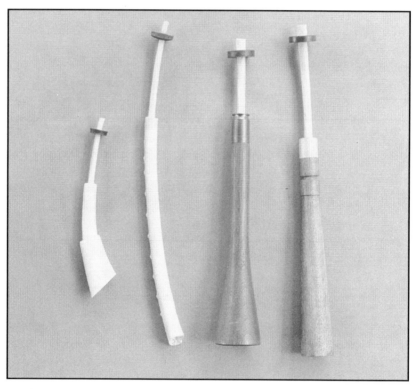

Fig. 6.6. *More yelpers, left to right: small model with short piece of humerus, one with vulture ulna and turkey radius, and two trumpets with wooden bells*

Table 6.1. Tools and supplies for making wingbone yelpers

Knife	Flexible rubber washer for lip guide
Steel wool or equivalent	Smoking pipe cleaner
Dish detergent	Liquid laundry bleach or hydrogen
Metal file, fine saw,	peroxide
rotary tool, or other	Silicone adhesive, epoxy, or other glue
means of cutting bone	Cord or leather lace for lanyard
Small bottle brush or	
rifle bore brush	

The process will go smoothly if you follow this sequence: 1) remove the bones from the carcass and cut off most of the meat, 2) remove the bone joints, 3) force out the major content from the hollow bones, 4) boil the bones in soapy water, 5) swab them out again and scrape them, 6) remove the pithy deposits near the joints, 7) simmer them again in soapy water, 8) clean them thoroughly inside and out, 9) bleach them, and 10) cut them to final size.

Removing the bones

If the bird has been cooked, pull the bones off the carcass and remove the remaining meat and most of the cartilage. If the specimen has not been cooked, remove the wing at the joint between the humerus and ulna/radius and separate the ulna and radius bones from each other and from the rest of the wing with a knife. For a yelper with three bones, take also the humerus, the femur, or the tibiotarsus (Fig. 6.3).

Proceed by cutting and scraping most of the meat from the outside of the bones. The middle wing feathers, the *secondaries,* adhere stubbornly to the ulna in uncooked specimens—separate these feathers from the bone with a knife. The dots of gristle left on the raw ulna where the feathers were stuck can be scraped off later.

Cutting off the bone joints

Cut the joints off the bones with a hack saw, a rotary power tool such as a Dremel, a bench grinder, or the edge of a common bastard or tapered file.

To use a file, cut deep grooves around the joints (Fig. 6.7) and snap them off. Smooth the snapped-off ends with the flat side of the file (Fig. 6.8) or with sandpaper. See Figure 6.9 for the approximate cutting points of the finished bones.

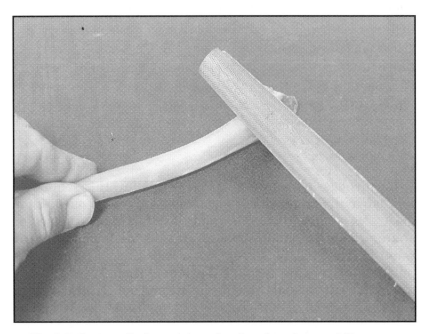

Fig. 6.7. Cutting off a bone joint using the edge of a metal file

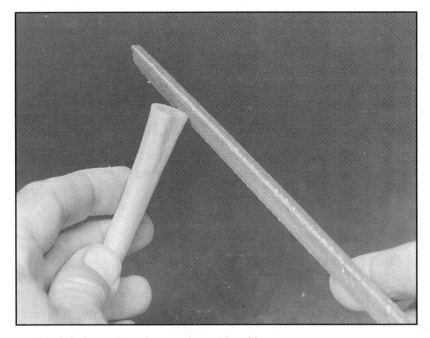

Fig. 6.8. Smoothing bone edge with a file

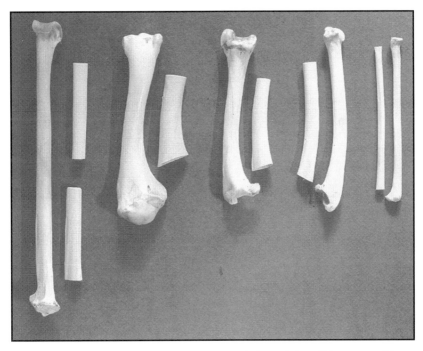

Fig. 6.9. Approximate cutting points, left to right: tibio-tarsus (drum bone), humerus, femur (thigh), ulna, and radius

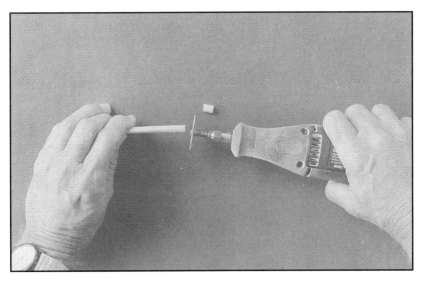

Fig. 6.10. Cutting off piece of radius bone to be used in making the lanyard

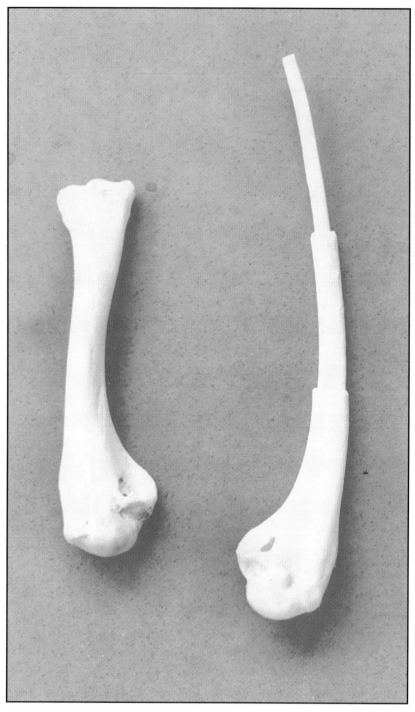

Fig. 6.11. *Unfinished humerus bone and yelper with humerus joint left on*

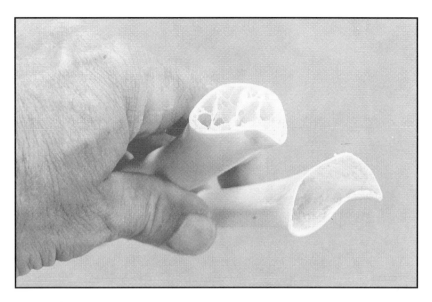

Fig. 6.12. *Two humerus bones, one with the bone network left in for strength and another with the interior bone removed. The bones can be used for yelpers either way.*

When you initially cut the joints off, leave more bone than you intend to use so that you have some leeway in sizing them later. At this stage, you are removing the joints mainly to reduce the bulk, get some of the bone marrow out, and get soapy water inside the bones.

Cut off and save a quarter-inch piece from the large end of the radius for use later in attaching the lanyard (Fig. 6.10).

The humerus can be used with the larger joint on or off (Fig. 6.11)—leaving the joint on makes a less fragile yelper. Some of the oldest wingbone yelpers were made that way. You can also cut off the large joint and leave the network of internal bone in place (Fig. 6.12). That will make a stronger bell on the finished product. The three alternative cuts of the humerus (joint left on, joint off with pithy bone left, and joint off with pithy bone removed) will result in only slight differences in tone, as will be discussed later.

Cleaning the bones

After removing the joints, run a brush, wire, or anything you can through the bones to push out their content. There won't be anything except a thin network of bone inside the humerus, but the radius, ulna, femur, and tibio-tarsus will contain marrow.

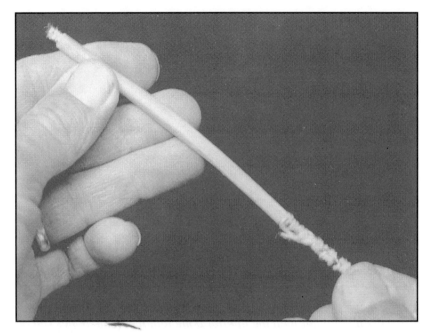

Fig. 6.13. *Cleaning inside the radius with a smoking pipe cleaner*

You won't be able to get all the marrow out at this stage, but getting the worst out and making a hole all the way through it will let the soap do its job.

Cover the bones with water, add a tablespoon of dishwashing detergent, and boil them gently for about an hour. Try removing the remaining meat from the outside with a knife. If you wish to test the flesh for doneness before the bones cool, to avoid burning yourself, hold the hot bone under running tap water while working with it. If the cooked meat does not come off easily, boil the bones longer.

When the meat comes off with reasonable ease, remove it and scrape the bones with a knife or steel wool. Blow the remaining content out of the hollow bones with your mouth, blast it out with a water pressure nozzle, or push it out with anything that you can get through the opening.

There is sometimes a spongy bone deposit blocking the hollow of the ulna on the larger end. If so, cut the pithy bone out with the point of a knife to make a hole so that you can remove the content of the bone, or cut off more of the bone at the joint to get past the pithy part. As you get into this, you'll see what I mean. If you don't find the end of the bone blocked, just move on to the next step.

Swab the inside of the radius with a smoking pipe cleaner. For the larger ulna, femur, and tibiotarsus, you will need a brush such as .22 caliber bore brush. A .30 caliber bore brush or a baby bottle nipple brush works well for cleaning out the femur. Nipple brushes from the grocery store also work well. If you use smoking pipe cleaners, the best is the rigid type with "bristles."

The humerus is an air sac bone and does not contain marrow or appreciable stain unless blood has entered through a wound. It does contain, however, a webwork of bone that can be removed by cutting or reaming with a small power tool. Or as previously mentioned, the large joint can be left on. If you remove the large joint of the humerus, you can either clean out the spongy bone at the end or leave it for strength (Fig. 6.12).

After removing most of the residue from the inside and the outside of the bones, place any stained bones back in a solution of dishwashing detergent and boil them gently for half an hour to loosen the remaining residue and fat. If fat is seen floating in the soapy solution, fix a fresh mixture and continue the boiling process.

After boiling, finish scraping the bones, inside and out. Use an awl, long screwdriver, or slender knife point to pick off any

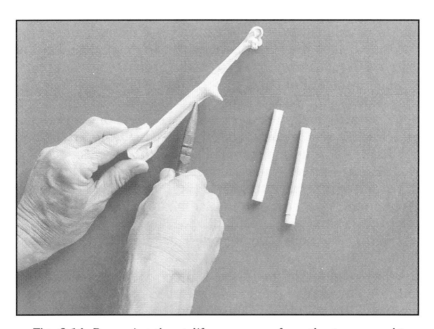

Fig. 6.14. *Removing the styliform process from the tarsus; and two finished tarsus bones ready to incorporate into a straight leg yelper*

dark spots that adhere to the inside of the bones. Some of the more obstinate cartilage and flesh can be cut and scraped off more easily after the bones dry.

To use the tarsometatarsus bone, cut the scaly skin from the lower leg with a knife and break off the spur and the sliver of bone it arises from (Fig. 6.14). The ridge is the *styliform process*. You will need to hone down the rough seam left on the bone where the styliform process was attached.

Bones can be partially cleaned by placing them in ant beds. Fire ants do a fair job, but will usually take three or four days. You must cover the ant bed in some way to keep roving animals from taking the bones.

Bone coloration

If the bones are still stained after scraping and the second boiling, as some will be, mix about one-quarter cup of laundry bleach in about a pint of soapy water and boil the bones gently for about ten minutes. Let the bones sit in the solution about thirty minutes as they cool, then rinse and dry them. The bones will become white as they dry. Caution: Leaving the bones in laundry bleach for more than an hour or two can damage the bone surface.

Hydrogen peroxide can be used in place of laundry bleach and is recommended because it will not damage the bone. Peroxide comes from the pharmacy or first aid section of the grocery. Use peroxide at full strength at room temperature.

Some discoloration is caused by deposits of fat sticking to the inside of the hollow bones. The oil may not appear on the bone surface until a few hours after the bone has been bleached. To remove oil spots, check inside the bone for small soft tissue deposits and chip them out with an awl, ice pick, or slender screwdriver. Then simmer the bones again in soapy water and permit them to soak in the soap solution for two or three hours. You may have to boil the bones several times to remove the very last spots of oil. Soaking in soapy water will not damage the bones, but long periods of boiling will damage them.

Leaving spots of oil discoloration does not affect the function of the yelper. I remove the oil spots only to create a more uniform color of the finished bone.

Bones come clean more easily when they are worked fresh. If you save bones unfrozen for long periods without cleaning them, oil and blood stains will be absorbed into the bone tissue. The stains can be removed by the bleaching and soaping processes, but with more difficulty than with fresh bones.

Domestic turkeys seem to have more unattractive bone discoloration than wild turkeys, probably due to their diet. Even wild turkeys sometimes have dark zones in their bones. These seem to be in definite regions such as at the large end of the femur. There are sometimes small blue-green stains, like copper sulfate. The blue-green stains are usually small and do not seriously detract from the appearance of the finished yelper.

One source of bone stain results from leaving the bones in a container made of an iron alloy. Rust stains can be scraped off with a knife, if they are not too deep, but can be avoided altogether by using a stainless steel pot. If you find rust stains, they can be removed by soaking briefly in lemon juice and table salt.

Bones are off-white, ivory, or straw colored, depending on the amount of bleaching. The more they are bleached, the whiter they will be. A few bones are naturally cream-colored and cannot be made pure white by bleaching. The off-white color is not objectionable.

Oil can be replaced in the bones to restore an old ivory color by simmering the bones gently a few minutes in cooking oil then washing them with soap. Since the oil-treated bones are translucent, any specks of residue inside can be seen through the bone. The degree of oil saturation can be adjusted by again simmering in soapy water to restore more opacity. Oil, or lack of it, in the bones does not affect the function of the yelper.

Assembling the bones

If you have never made a wingbone yelper, I suggest cleaning two sets of bones. Finish your first yelper before working with the other set, making any improvements in technique that are needed when you make the second yelper.

Even if you don't plan to use the humerus, femur, or tibiotarsus, you should clean and save them—you will be able to use them later if you decide to expand your horizons as a yelper maker and user.

After the bones have been cut to proper length, bevel the edges to give them a more finished look. Do the beveling with

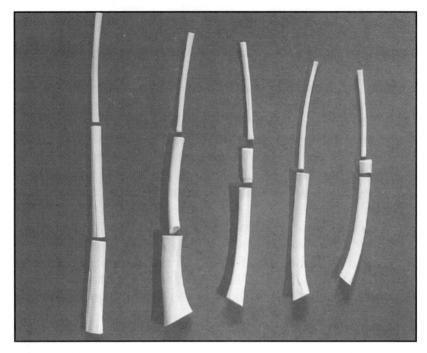

Fig. 6.15. *Bones for the yelper models shown in Fig. 6.2, cut and ready to assemble*

a power tool, sandpaper, or a file. This is the last step before assembling the bones with glue.

If you removed a quarter-inch section of the radius for the lanyard as suggested, you will probably need to trim the radius further only at mouth end. The ulna will usually need to be shortened by about one-half inch from the small end and will need to be shaped on the larger end. Look at the photos of my yelpers to see the sizes and shapes to aim for.

Select the model you wish to make, then size and finish the bones. Position the bones before gluing them to be sure everything fits and looks right. You will have to cut off small pieces or hone down parts to get some of them to fit properly. If a small bone fits loosely into a larger one, it will be tight after the glue dries.

Notice how certain positions and bone combinations produce more graceful configurations than others. Using the radius and ulna from the same wing makes a more graceful curve, but cross-matched bones are just as functional.

If you have a supply of bones from different turkeys, you will find that some bones fit together better than others.

Sometimes a radius bone can be inserted into the ulna and rotated slightly to make a firm connection.

Use a glue that has enough bulk to plug the spaces where the bones do not fit snugly. Ordinary "super glue" is not satisfactory—it is good for gluing your fingers together but has no bulk, and its strength is greatly overrated. Epoxy glues are good. I especially like Devcon's five-minute epoxy and their other adhesives. There are many adhesives on the market. Check a large craft supply store.

I suggest using clear silicone or raw rubber cement as an adhesive for your first yelper. Tacky glue, such as silicone, will hold the bones and fill the spaces in one application. Bones glued with silicone can be pulled apart and reglued to permit you to experiment with different bone combinations or to correct errors. Pulling a yelper apart and regluing wastes only a dab of silicone, and it may teach you something of value as you experiment.

If the bones should come apart while in use, a yelper made with silicone or rubber cement will usually continue to function satisfactorily if you stick the bones back together. You can reglue the bones later.

If you want a more permanent connection than silicone or rubber cement can give, use epoxy to fix the bones, then fill any open spaces between the bones with silicone or cement after the glue dries.

Single bone model. A gobbler radius bone makes a good single bone yelper. Simply cut off the joints of the radius as you would for any other yelper and clean out the bone. Use the flatter end of the radius as the mouthpiece. Do not shorten the bone as much as you would for a multi-bone model.

When the radius bone alone is used as a yelper, you have to cup your hands properly, as explained later.

Two-bone model. The radius will be the mouthpiece, as in all wingbone yelpers, to which will be glued one of the larger bones. The classic two-bone model employs the radius with either the ulna or femur. Actually, the radius mouthpiece can be combined with any larger bone or other component, such as a wooden bell or cow horn, to make a yelper.

Test fit the radius into the ulna or femur (Fig. 6.16). The radius will sometimes slip in easily but jam tightly when pushed further or rotated. Use that to advantage before applying glue, but be careful not to use too much force when

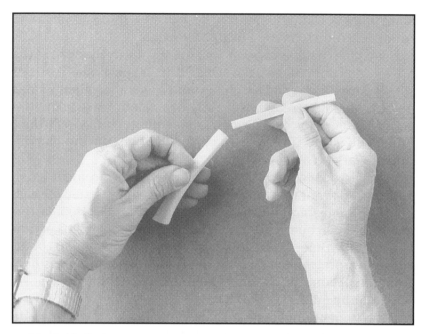

Fig. 6.16. *Radius bone being fitted into ulna to make a 2-bone model*

you twist the bones—force from inside will crack a hollow bone with surprising ease.

If you were able to get the mouthpiece to bind with the ulna as described, be sure the final position is the one you want. The angle at which the radius binds is not always the best configuration aesthetically.

When you are ready to assemble the yelper, coat about half an inch of the round end of the radius with cement, silicone, or epoxy, then stick it about two-thirds of an inch into the ulna (Fig. 6.16). If using epoxy, allow it to become slightly tacky before applying so that it will not run excessively. If some of the adhesive oozes out, push it back into the crevices where the bones join and wipe away the excess from the outside. Test for blockage by blowing breath through the yelper. If silicone or glue gets into the hole of the radius, use a smoking pipe cleaner to clear the opening before the adhesive dries.

If the mouthpiece fits loosely into the end of the ulna, you will need to permit the glue to dry in the preferred position. Using tacky glue and sticking the yelper straight up to dry usually works well. Keep an eye on the yelper as it dries and make any necessary adjustments in the position of the bones before the glue becomes too firm.

Another way to join the radius to the other bone is with a small piece of plastic tubing (Fig. 6.17). Heat a one-half-inch piece of vinyl tubing in hot water to make it flexible and force it onto the round end of the radius. While the plastic is still warm and flexible, force the end of the radius with the tubing into the small end of the ulna. The radius should stick snugly in the ulna when it cools.

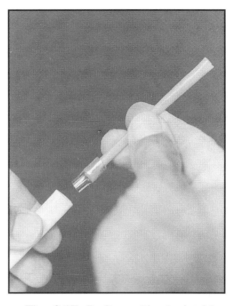

Fig. 6.17. Radius with vinyl tubing on round end ready to insert into ulna

The plastic tubing is especially useful when the radius is much smaller than the ulna—it helps give a tight fit. The main problem with the tubing is that a single size of plastic tubing does not fit all bone sizes and different tubing sizes are hard to find.

Three-bone models.   The three-bone design uses the radius as the mouthpiece, another bone in the middle, and a larger bone attached to the end. The humerus is traditionally used as the large bone, but the femur or the large end of the ulna can also be used. Look at the photographs for the general idea. The process is somewhat like making a two-bone model and sticking a third larger bone on the end.

A yelper made with the humerus as the third bone will produce acceptable tones without cupping your hands because the sound is amplified by the large bone like the bell of a musical horn. However, tone is improved by cupping the hands.

If you opt to leave the joint on the humerus (Fig. 6.11), the small hole that naturally occurs in the large end should be reamed open a little more than it already is.

A small gobbler ulna works well as the middle bone with the femur as the third, but the ulna will need to be cut to size. The ulna of a hen will usually fit properly into the ulna of a gobbler. Try the combinations and make any necessary alterations to the bones before gluing.

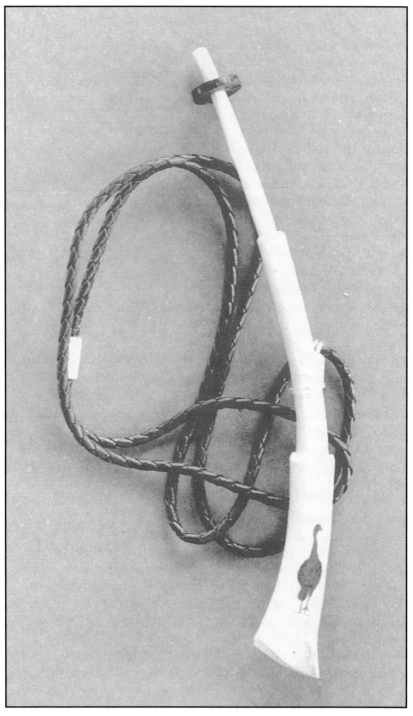

Fig. 6.18. *The "Hermit" yelper with lanyard, mouthpiece, and artwork*

Epoxy or other strong glue should be used where a rigid fit is needed, as in the three-bone model in which the middle bone piece has been worked to fit less than one-half-inch deep. When epoxy glue is used, the spaces may require further filling with silicone sealant. When there is ample bone overlap, as between the radius and ulna, silicone alone will hold quite well.

I usually glue the largest and middle bones together first. After two hours, silicone or epoxy will be dry enough to add the radius as the mouthpiece.

There is some latitude in the length to cut the bones, in the size and shapes of the openings, and in how far down to insert the bones into each other. I make yelpers with a large number of finished bones before me so that I can mix and match before gluing a set together. You will not have as many options unless you save the bones from several turkeys.

Most large yelpers, such as those made with the humerus, cow horns, and wooden bells, make louder sounds at a lower pitch than smaller yelpers. They have a mellow tone and sound more like a gobbler's voice. Such yelpers make especially good long distance callers to stimulate "shock gobbling" in spring and for gobbler hunting in fall.

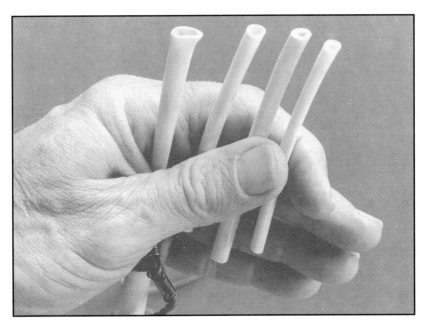

Fig. 6.19. *Mouthpieces illustrating variation in opening size. The bone on the far left is too flat across and needs to be trimmed to more closely resemble the others.*

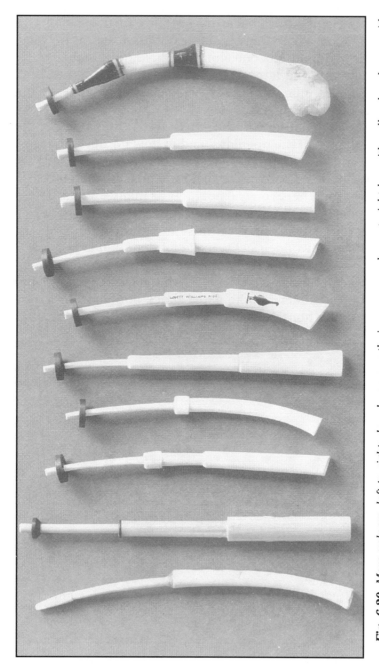

Fig. **6.20.** *More yelpers, left to right: deer bone mouthpiece, cane yelper, straight leg with collar, hen bones with collar, standard straight leg, standard 3-bone with inscriptions, straight leg variant, 2-bone straight leg, standard 2-bone, and 3-bone variant with trim*

Other models. Any of the turkey's hollow bones can be incorporated into a yelper. You will need to cut and shape some bones to make them fit and may need to hone down or open up others depending on the combination you seek. With a little imagination, you can come up with a unique design of your own.

I made a "double barrel" cow horn model with both large and small diameter mouthpieces that makes either gobbler or hen tones depending on which of the two mouthpieces is used (Fig. 6.21). For this type, two mouthpieces are inserted into a piece cut from the upper part of the tibiotarsus (drum bone) and the tibiotarsus is inserted into a drilled-out hole in the end of a small cow horn. I don't use it much, but it illustrates what you can do with a few bones and an open mind.

I made a good yelper by combining a Gould's turkey radius, an osceola ulna, and part of a femur of a mountain lion I found dead on a Gould's hunt in Mexico (Fig. 6.22). I have yelpers made of components of all five wild turkey subspecies and one made from the femur of a lamb we BBQ'd in camp on a hunting trip in Mexico.

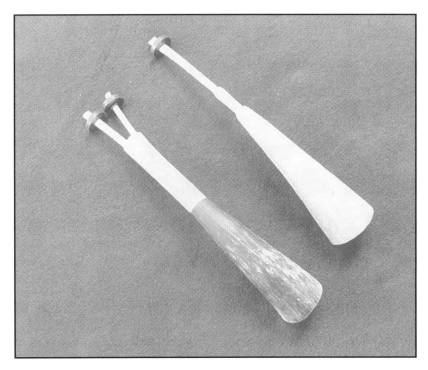

Fig. 6.21. *Yelpers with cow horn sounding bells*

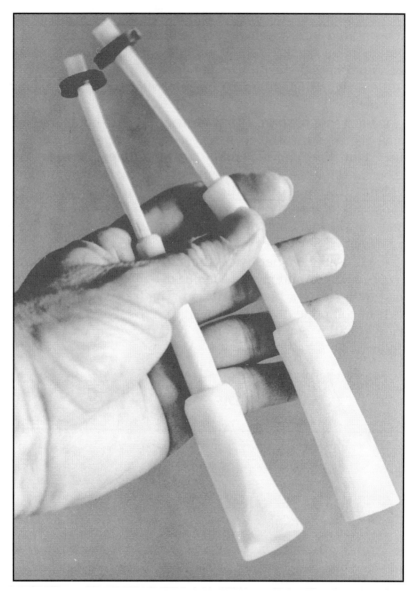

Fig. 6.22. *Yelpers made with mountain lion and lamb femurs. Both have Gould's wild turkey radii as mouthpieces.*

You can use a piece of the tarsometarsus—the bone of the scaly lower leg—and a piece of the femur to make a "Straight Leg" yelper (Fig. 6.20). Another variation in Figure 6.20 has a small collar to give it a more finished look. You can dress a yelper with a collar at the junction of any two bones or anywhere else a collar will fit.

Another way of joining the radius to a larger bone employs a modified brass rifle hull (Fig. 6.23). The calibers that fit best are .222 and .223, but others may work depending on the size of the bones.

Cut off the brass base using the tool with which you cut the bone joints. Insert the large end of the brass into the small end of the ulna. If the ulna is too small for the insertion, ream it out. If that appears infeasible, try sticking the bone inside the brass. If the big end of the brass and the bone are the same size, insert a short piece of plastic tubing inside the bone and insert the other end of the tubing inside the brass like an inside sleeve. Finish by inserting and gluing the radius into the small end of the rifle hull.

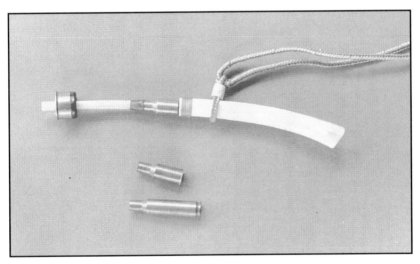

Fig. 6.23. *Rifle brass and yelper made with rifle brass ("Spirit" yelper by Parker Whedon)*

Finishing Touches

As the silicone dries, remove the excess from around the joined bones by wiping with a paper towel. If it dries before you can remove it, cut off the excess with a knife and rub the thin layer off the bone surface with your fingers. It is much easier to wipe away the excess adhesive before it dries completely. Epoxy reaches a flexible plastic state in which it can be cut with a knife or scissors. Check the instructions on the container for drying and working time and use that information to advantage.

If you are using rifle brass as described above, you can dress the outside of the joints with twine or other material (Fig. 6.23) and coat the wrapping with a strong clear glue or epoxy.

A neck lanyard and adjustable lip guide are needed to complete the yelper. Any small diameter cord can be used as a lanyard. Bulky material such as braided cloth or leather boot laces are good. Large craft shops have a wide selection of suitable lace materials to choose from.

Loop the lanyard material around your neck to get it the right length before cutting it. You will need about one yard per lanyard. You should be able to stick the yelper in a shirt pocket without taking the lanyard from your neck.

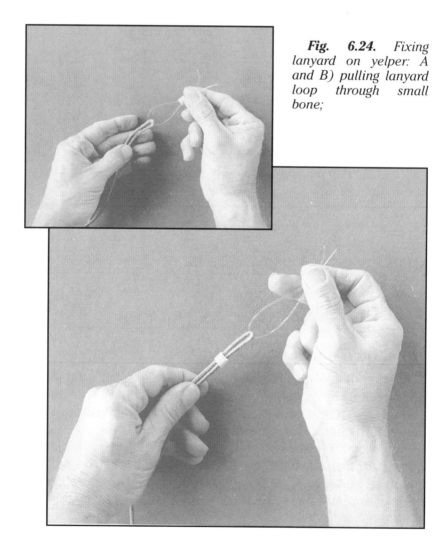

Fig. 6.24. Fixing lanyard on yelper: A and B) pulling lanyard loop through small bone;

One way to attach the lanyard is with a small hollow section of bone cut from the round end of the radius (Fig. 6.10). Use a piece of small line to pull a loop of lanyard material thorough the hollow of the small piece of bone (Fig. 6.24A & 6.24B). Then place the lace loop around the yelper and snug the small piece of bone tightly against the yelper. Secure it with a simple overhand knot (Fig. 6.24C & 6.24D). Tie a knot in the loose ends to close the lanyard and trim off the excess. If the connection loosens at the yelper end, simply tighten the overhand knot to make it snug again.

A large glass bead, a small piece of cane, a .22 rifle brass with the base cut off, or any other short tube can be substituted for the bone piece to secure the lanyard to the yelper. You can also use a device that comes with eye glass lanyards or buy a ready made yelper lanyard.

C and D) tightening lanyard on yelper

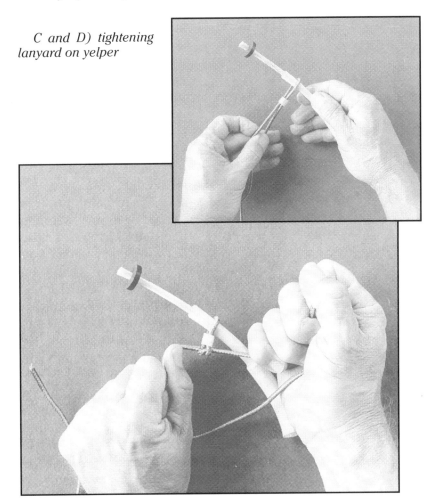

You can have a leather shop make a belt scabbard for your wingbone yelper (Fig. 6.25) or you can use a pencil clip (Fig. 6. 26) to carry the yelper in a shirt pocket.

For a lip guide, use a flexible three-eighths-inch black rubber plumbing washer. You can make a fixed lip guide by gluing on a stiff washer or by wrapping cord in place and coating it with glue. Otherwise use any small disc with a hole in it—bottle cork is often used. Some of the old homemade yelper models used rubber test tube stoppers (Fig. 6.27) of the type available in hobby shops, but they are too bulky for my taste. The rubber of test tube stoppers is flexible, however, and you can slice off washer sized discs if you cannot find a flexible plumbing washer.

I usually leave the bone surface more or less natural by merely scraping any discolored spots and lightly sanding, but you can take the finishing process further with wet sanding and polishing to make the bone look like ivory if you have the tools and the inclination. If you'd rather, you can find a scrimshaw craftsman to finish the bone to look like ivory. He can add your name and artwork too.

The bone can be left its natural off-white color or it can be dyed. If the bones are to be lettered with India ink, scrimshawed, or engraved, you

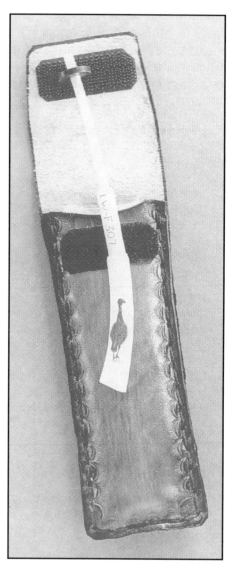

Fig. 6.25. *Leather scabbard for a wingbone yelper*

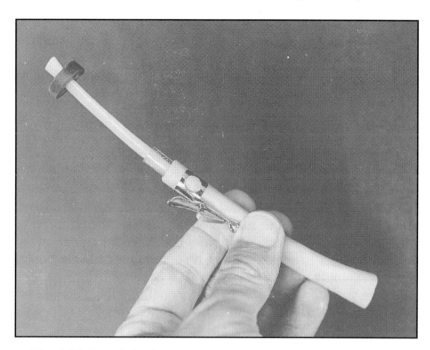

Fig. 6.26. *Pencil clip for carrying yelper in shirt pocket*

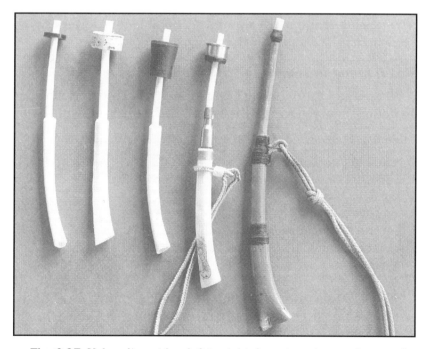

Fig. 6.27. *Yelper lip guides, left to right: faucet washer, cork, test tube stopper, shotgun shell base, twine wrap*

need to prepare the surface by sanding with very small grit paper or wet sanding. You can soak the bone in acetone to remove any surface oil that would cause a problem in lettering. An epoxy or clear varnish coating will preserve the lettering and strengthen the bone. You can buy coatings, inks, and dyes at craft shops.

Using the Wingbone Yelper

Sound is made by sucking air into the mouth through the yelper. Most people make their first sounds by smacking with tight lips like making a loud mock kiss.

If you ever played a woodwind or brass musical instrument, you didn't learn without making a lot of noise at first. So it is with the wingbone turkey yelper—you have to smack away until you begin to make sounds resembling a turkey's voice. Work on yelping notes first.

Before you start the noise, look through the next few pages. Don't attempt to learn it all at one time. You can't. Try to accomplish each step before spending much time on the next and occasionally review the steps you have passed to see how you are progressing. When you tire of practicing, find something else to do and resume practice later.

You can learn to make sounds acceptable to wild turkeys in a few hours of serious effort.

Seven steps in learning

When I tutor the use of the wingbone yelper, I use the following procedure in seven steps (Table 6.2). Each step is essential.

Table 6.2. Steps in mastering the wingbone turkey yelper.

1. Hold the instrument correctly
2. Know the sounds to imitate
3. Make the first sounds
4. Improve tonal quality
5. Control the sounds
6. Use the yelper in hunting
7. Aim toward mastery

Step 1. Hold the instrument correctly. Hand position is critical. With three-bone yelpers employing the humerus or femur, and with trumpets and models with sounding bells, you can get by without cupping both hands, but even those sound better with the hands cupped over the end of the bell.

Hold the hands as shown in Figure 6.28. Place the end of the yelper at the edge of your palm between the thumb and first finger (Fig. 6.28A). Curl the first finger in toward the butt of the thumb to close the space between them (Fig. 6.28B) and place the other hand so that its thumb lies next to and parallel to the other thumb, closing the space between them. Then close the fingers to block the gap between the left thumb and other left fingers (Fig. 6.28C). Curl the other left fingers together to complete the cup, and make any final adjustments necessary to close up the cup and to allow you to reach the mouthpiece of the yelper with your lips (Fig. 6.28D).

You will see small variations in hand positions from one hunter to another, but the principle is the same—make a cone with both hands to amplify and modulate the sound. Leave the end of the cupped hands open. It will seem awkward at first but do not neglect this step. It will soon seem natural.

Step 2. Know the sounds to imitate. You already know what a turkey sounds like. If you need models, experienced turkey hunters can demonstrate turkey sounds for you.

The best learning cassettes on the market are my Real Turkeys™ recordings, which contain examples of both hens and gobblers of all age classes recorded in the wild. More than sixty thousand have been sold. I narrate the tapes with special attention to the calls used in hunting. Ask for Real Turkeys™ audiocassettes at your hunting supply dealer or contact me for ordering information.

Step 3. Make the first sounds. Sound is made by the vibration of your lips as you draw air across them. The smacking sounds of a mock kiss become the sounds of a wild turkey's voice when made through the yelper. It will be difficult to make any sound at all when you first try, and when you finally get a sound, the notes will have a harsh smacking quality. As soon as you can make almost-turkey-like sounds, you are ready for Step 4.

Step 4. Improve tonal quality. When you learned to play the trumpet, you didn't begin with "The Flight of the Bumblebee" or the guitar with "Malaguena." You started with simple exercises and learned to make the sound and tonal sequences. Learning the wingbone works the same way. Practice tonal control before you practice a variety of turkey calls.

The way to make immediate improvement in tone is to practice making longer notes. Long notes will not sound like a

Fig. 6.28. Steps in correct hand positions for using the wingbone yelper: A) tip of yelper goes between thumb and forefinger;

B) hand partially closed;

C) other hand fitted to the first with fingers closing all holes;

D) yelper raised to lips (Photos Sandra Prescott)

turkey, but as you make one-second-long sustained notes, you will stop smacking and will gain control of the tone. In time, you will be able to soften the sounds and make notes of any length you wish.

Try making notes of various pitch and tonal quality without necessarily sounding like a turkey. You will find that you can make notes at different pitches and will develop a wide range of tonal control. Begin with a low note, then higher, and so on until you reach the high kee-kee-like notes. Then start with high notes and come down the scale. Try to hit various intermediate pitches. Use this exercise from time to time to improve lip control.

Look in a mirror as you practice. Observe that when you call with a smacking technique, you do so by lowering your jaw abruptly. That briefly makes more space inside your mouth, which creates a partial vacuum and causes air to rush through the yelper and across your lips to make the sound. But as you smack, your lips open and that terminates the vacuum and ends the tone. Thus, smacking makes only short notes with little lip control.

When you make longer notes in practice, you will use your throat as well as your jaw and you won't drop your jaw abruptly. You will do that without thinking about it. Your lips will stay put and the partial vacuum in your buccal cavity will persist as you make the call. You will be swallowing the air taken in with each yelp to maintain the same level of vacuum in your mouth. You will find it natural to breathe through your nose as you yelp that way.

Step 4 is important even for many long-time wingbone users and for those who have given up the wingbone as a lost cause. You will make strides in mastering the wingbone as soon as you begin to master long notes and stop smacking.

Step 5. Control the sounds. Volume is controlled by the amount of force used in drawing in air. Pitch is controlled by the tightness of the lips. Pitch and tonal quality are also affected by the depth of the mouthpiece in the lips, the place the mouthpiece enters the lips, and the angle the instrument is held.

Try placing the mouthpiece in different spots on your lips as you practice. Find a position that feels right. If your lips begin to fatigue, move the mouthpiece to another spot on your lips. If you use another spot enough, it too will begin to feel right.

You will make a few foul notes, most likely the first one or two notes when you begin a call, as you would when learning on any turkey yelper or musical instrument. Consistency will come with practice. In the meantime, be assured that the turkeys don't mind the sour notes.

The fastest way to gain tonal consistency is to practice often for short periods—two or three minutes at a time once or twice a week is better than trying to hold out for an hour or two a few days before the hunting season opens.

Why brief sessions? Because the more practice you get in making the first note, the better you will get at starting out cold without making a bad first note. You can only start out cold one time each practice session. So do more, but briefer, sessions.

If your first note is not quite up to par, make the first sound at low volume then increase the volume as the tone improves with the next few notes. The turkey won't hear the first notes, but even if he does, he won't care.

When you can pick up the yelper and make a good sound on the first try, you are getting there. That will happen eventually.

Step 6. Use the yelper in hunting. After you can make turkey-like sounds, even if imperfect and without consistency, go to the woods and use your yelper in hunting. Do not hesitate to call often and try to imitate every turkey call you hear.

Turkeys are tolerant of excessive calling by other turkeys and have no idea that the human predator has learned to imitate their voice. Yelp as much as you wish. The more you yelp, the sooner you will master the wingbone yelper.

You never know when a turkey will respond to random yelping and the thought that a turkey might be listening strengthens your calling motivation. When hunting, I usually call about every three to five minutes, sometimes more often, whether I have heard a turkey or not, and get my best sustained practice that way.

The best calling experience is gained when you call turkeys in fall and winter. That's when you can talk **to** and **with** the turkeys instead of only **at** them. If there is no fall hunting season where you live, you can practice calling fall turkeys without shooting them. That's even more productive than hunting because you don't terminate your calling session by shooting and you get to observe turkeys and their calling more closely. Fall calling technique is explained in my book *The Voice and Vocabulary of the Wild Turkey*.

Fig. 6.29. *Useful aids for learning to call turkeys—Real Turkeys™ cassettes and the book,* The Voice and Vocabulary of the Wild Turkey

Step 7. Aim toward mastery. After basic skill and initial confidence are developed, keep trying to improve on small flaws in technique and work on a wider variety of calls. Don't listen to other callers too long without checking back with the turkeys in the woods or listening to a good recording.

Keep yourself challenged as you learn but don't rush it. Development of skill requires the passage of time as well as practice. I think the human nervous system works on projects between practice sessions and probably even while we sleep. No matter how long or intensely you practice, you can't move forward faster than time will permit. Keep a yelper handy. When you see it, you will be reminded to practice.

Using the lip guide

The small disc on the mouthpiece is useful in positioning the lips and creating airtight lip contact. I position the rubber disc about three-eighths of an inch down the mouthpiece and move it in or out as needed. Pushing the lips lightly against the guide flattens and tenses the lip muscles, which favorably affects tonal quality.

Some trumpet and wingbone yelpers have lip guides fixed permanently in position on the mouthpiece. If you have such a yelper and want the lip guide in a different place, you may be able to substitute a flexible rubber washer. If the fixed lip guide is too far from the end, it may be feasible to add a washer to close the distance or you may be able to cut off a small piece of the mouthpiece tip to shorten the distance to the lip guide.

Calls you can make on the wingbone

As soon as you can make any turkey-like sounds, you will be able to yelp and cluck and soon after will be making the calls in Table 6.3. The only well-known turkey calls that are not adaptable to the wingbone are gobbling and purring, but a few hunters can do both on the wingbone. Neither call is necessary in hunting, however.

You can call turkeys successfully in spring and fall by using only the plain yelp. The yelping calls are made up of the standard notes you have already been working on. If you can plain yelp, you can also lost yelp. The only difference between the plain yelp and lost yelp is that the lost yelp is louder and longer.

To cluck, simply smack a very short, sharp note. Another way to cluck is to place your tongue on the tip of the mouthpiece and draw it away smartly while drawing in air. Don't be concerned about your clucking sounding like alarm putting. A putt only makes a turkey look up. He won't likely leave when he hears it unless he sees danger. Some clucks sound exactly like putts, even to turkeys.

Table 6.3. Calls made on the wingbone yelper in order of difficulty[a]

Call	Peculiar character, if any
Plain cluck	Short, staccato notes widely separated
Plain yelp	4-7 yelping notes, low to moderate volume
Lost yelp	8-50 yelping notes, loud volume
Tree yelp	3-5 yelping notes, nasal tone, low volume
1- or 2-note yelp	Only 1 or 2 brief yelp notes in the series
Cutting	2-30+ loud clucks with irregular rhythm
Kee-kee	3-4 whistle-like notes with musical effect
Kee-kee-run	A kee-kee preceded, or followed, by yelping

[a] For a list of the entire vocabulary and call characteristics, see *The Voice and Vocabulary of The Wild Turkey* (Williams, 1984).

The kee-kee and kee-kee-run require different lip action, but are not difficult to master on the wingbone. To make kee-kee tones, make your lips tight to create very high, squeaking sounds. Once you attain high whistle-like tones, even if you can't control them, you are on the way. Keep trying until you get it right and practice briefly, but often, to gain consistency.

A tree yelp is a subdued three to four note yelp of low volume and a nasal quality. Turkeys make tree yelps with their bills nearly closed. To make a tree yelp with your wingbone, emulate the turkeys by covering the end of the yelper with part of a hand. Try for a short, low, muffled, nasal quality yelp. Three-bone yelpers made with the large joint of the humerus left uncut make good tree yelps.

A few more pointers

The process of drawing in air with the throat muscles, learned by practicing long notes, must be stressed. Wingbone users can call turkeys by the smacking mode, but that is only because lonely and horny turkeys are so forgiving. The difference between smacking and yelping is like the difference between dog paddling and swimming. Your calling success will improve by learning to use your throat as explained in Step 4.

Tone is affected by several things. One is the way the tip of the mouthpiece is cut. I find that kee-keeing is easier and more consistent with the mouthpiece cut flat across the lip end as most mouthpieces are. Some other sounds are better made on slightly rounded mouthpiece tips. You can make modifications in the shape of the mouthpiece in small increments by using a file or sandpaper. Find out for yourself the shapes that work best for you.

Many homemade wingbone yelpers have the mouthpiece (radius) cut off flat and too wide at the lip end. It is better to cut off the radius joints so that the mouthpiece is not much wider than the rest of the bone.

Making raspy versus clear tones depends on the way the mouthpiece fits into your lips. Raspiness seems to be most pronounced when the tip is in contact with the softer parts inside the lips. Although wild turkeys sometimes sound raspy, raspiness is not an important tonal quality for hunting.

An important tone factor is the depth the mouthpiece is inserted into the other bone. Generally, the deeper it is inserted, the higher the pitch. Also, the total length of the yelper, all bones considered, is a factor—the longer the instrument, the deeper the tone usually is. That has to do with tonal resonance and is very complicated. I know little about that; I get the tones I am after by testing yelpers as I make them. I am sometimes surprised to hear the tones certain bone combinations produce.

Some wingbone yelpers sound like gobblers, some more like fall jakes, and some more like hens. Hardly any two sound exactly alike. Subtleties in tonal quality will become more noticeable as you gain experience and you will gain more control over the tones as you master the wingbone.

In fall hunting, I mostly use a yelper that makes jake-like tones because I am calling male turkeys that are looking for male companionship. I also have a yelper on which it is easy to kee-kee. This yelper is especially useful in hunting jakes in fall. In spring, I use mostly a hen-sounding yelper to interest gobblers who are looking for hens, and I sometimes use a gobbler yelp on a "hung up" spring gobbler. Using several yelpers is not very important to hunting success, but it's easy to do and I enjoy the dimension of versatility that two or three yelpers provide.

Confidence is important. As you develop calling skill, the improvement you see will increase your confidence and that will further your incentive to use your wingbone yelper. Try your wingbone in hunting even if you think some of your other yelpers sound better. When you bag your first gobbler using your wingbone yelper, you won't need any more confidence-boosting and you won't need your other yelpers anymore.

7

Photographing and Recording

Anybody who can shoot a gun can work a modern camera. Snapshot cameras are so inexpensive and easy to use that there is no reason not to take reams of pictures of your hunting trips and your trophies. Videography and sound recording are also within reach. Photography and audio recording can be new dimensions to your turkey hunting.

In this chapter I will explain how to make good photographs of your hunt and your trophy. I will also provide a little information about photographing and recording live turkeys.

Photographing a Trophy

If you don't have a snapshot camera, buy a simple, inexpensive, automatic one with a built-in flash. Get one that will fit into your coat pocket and take it on every hunting trip. You can get a good one for less than $75. Disposable cameras are perfect for hunting and fishing trips when a better camera might be at risk. Get one with a built-in flash for around $10. I use professional photography equipment almost every day, but I also have a simple snapshot camera and disposable cameras. I find them indispensable for what they are designed for.

If you are not already familiar with the general use of cameras, you need a handbook on photography fundamentals. Get the smallest, simplest book you can find. I will not go into photography in general, but here's how to take a good snapshot picture.

Take a little time to look at some old snapshots you have on file and see what is good and what is bad about them. You can learn from your mistakes and do an increasingly better job with your turkey pictures.

The trophy is dead. It is time to take a few pictures. In many cases they will soon be all you'll have left of the hunt.

You should have taken pains not to mess up the trophy hauling it around, but it probably needs a little grooming. Wipe excessive blood from its head. Straighten any messed up feathers. Stretch the wings and the tail open so you can see more of the beautiful bird.

Pick a good place to take the picture and look through the camera viewfinder at what's in front of the camera. Don't just look at the subject—your eyes have a way of automatically ignoring what doesn't count, but the camera won't do that. Everything you see in the viewfinder will be in the picture. Some of what you see you don't need in the photo. The best trophy photos show the hunter still wearing hunting clothing, the turkey, the hunter's gun, and the setting where the bird was taken. Add a large rock or photogenic log or tree and you have a picture. The background, surroundings, and distance to the subject are critical.

Distance. Get very close to the subject. Fill the viewfinder to the edges with the subject matter you want. You don't need a person's feet in the picture and the photo will not benefit from having blank space around the subject. Concentrate on the face of the hunter and the trophy. Be sure the eyes of both are in focus.

Fig. 7.1. Hunter in traditional pose with trophy turkey: A) camera farther from subject;

B) camera closer. Which looks best?

Fig. 7.2. Author posing with a Gould's gobbler at the exact location of the kill, within five minutes after shooting. A real memory jogger.

Background. Try to get the trophy and hunter outlined against a natural and uncluttered background. One way to do that is to find a place with open space behind the subject. Pay attention to anything that is directly behind the turkey or the hunter's head—cluttered backgrounds detract seriously from otherwise good photographs.

Lighting. Contrary to popular opinion, the best light is not from the front. It is from the side or behind. Thin shade or a lightly overcast sky makes better light for photography than bright sunlight. Lighting angles and light color in midmorning and midafternoon are better than midday.

Be sure the hunter's hat is back on his head so that his face will not be heavily shaded. Just raise the cap brim a little, but do not have the hunter squinting into the bright sun. Use the flash to light the shadows and creases in the face.

If you do not have an automatic camera, shoot at least three exposures of what you want. Change the f-stop to one notch above and one below the best setting to "bracket" the target, as professional photographers and artillery gunners do. You will get at least one picture with a correct exposure. If you use a built-in camera flash, you do not need to bracket the exposure in this manner—the light from the flash is adjusted automatically. Be sure to use the flash whether you think it is needed or not. It won't cause overexposure.

Fig. 7.3. Face shading: A) hunters' faces shaded;

B) the same shot ten seconds later with fill-in flash

Surroundings. The hunting jeep, swamp buggy, or horse will add interest to the photo if photographed in the woods, but don't try to get the whole thing in the picture. Just enough to tell what it is. If there is an old rail fence, large tree stump, boulder, or other photogenic landmark nearby, get part of it in the picture, but avoid extraneous objects that had nothing to do with the hunt or the setting.

There is probably no better place to photograph a recently killed turkey than the spot where it was taken and no better time than immediately after the kill. Looking back at such a photo will jolt one's memory like nothing else can.

The worst possible hunting photo is one with your garage, house, driveway, mama's best rose bush, or the family dog in the picture. If you want to make a trophy picture positively awful, include all the above plus take a shower, comb your hair, shave, and change clothes for the occasion.

Composition. In posing the bird, spread the tail and wings. Pose one shot holding it by the legs (not the neck) and stretch the wings so that they make the bird look big, limp, and freshly taken. Try laying the bird with wings and tail partly spread on a log or stump, and kneel beside or behind it.

Fig. 7.4. *Photo on thinly overcast day with sun behind subjects. Fill-in flash was not needed because shadows were not strong.*

Sometimes a photo looks best if the hunter is examining the bird instead of looking at the camera. Put on a smile to reveal your satisfaction. Don't look too serious—you did it for fun and it may appear that you regret killing the poor bird if you are too solemn.

After everything is set up, don't stop with only one or two pictures. Take several shots, changing the camera angle and hunter's position and/or posture. Walk around on the other side and have the hunter turn too. Shoot with hat on and with it off. I promise that you will be pleasantly surprised with some of the shots you did not expect to be good.

Fig. 7.5. *Hunter unloading his Florida turkey from a swamp buggy*

Table 7.1 is a list of tips that will improve your snapshots. Here are the errors hunter photographers often make.

• Camera too far from the subject. Remedy: Get close.

• Cluttered background. Remedy: Look behind the subject before shooting.

• Uncertain lighting conditions. Remedy: Use built-in flash.

• Poor focus. Remedy: Take several shots, refocus each time.

• Unpleasant facial expressions. Remedy: Tell the subject he's ugly.

• Mouth full of cigarette or chewing tobacco. Remedy: Tell the subject you will show his doctor the picture.

Some of your best hunting photos will not be posed and may not emphasize the trophy. Take a few shots of party members relaxing near the campfire, somebody making a toast to the successful hunt, setting up camp, eating, or other candid shots.

Table 7.1. Tips on photographing your trophy and hunt

Equipment

Simple, small, automatic 35mm camera with built-in flash

Fast color print film—ASA 200 or faster

Time delay and tripod so that nobody has to be behind the camera

The Scene

Take photos in woods; use camp and woodland backgrounds

Avoid carports, houses, cars, yard dogs and other domestic objects

Hold turkey by legs rather than neck

Arrange tail and wings attractively over log or on ground

Place cap back to throw daylight on face; or shoot without cap

Get close to subject; you don't need hunter's whole body in photo

Props

Wear hunting clothing and hold gun

Include photogenic hunting truck, if used

Include whole hunting group in some photos

Other

Take several photos, changing focus, f-stop, and speed

Use flash even in daylight to fill in dark spots in scene

Take photos with subject smiling

Photograph people and activities to document hunt

Take photos while subjects are unaware

When you are grand slam hunting, you may not know exactly where you are in relation to the rest of the world. Buy a local map and find out. Mark up the map and save it. Make entries on the map and in your hunting diary to permit you to retrace your itinerary by dates. Mark your photos with enough information to identify their content. Write lightly on the edge of the photo backs.

Use a standard lined record book for a few hunting notes. If you get behind in making entries, catch up one rainy day from memory. Don't worry about missing information—anything is better than nothing and you may be surprised how vivid your memory is if you don't wait too long.

Close-ups. If your turkey is a freak or has bragging trophy features, be sure to photograph the features of interest very close up. Get as close as a snapshot camera will focus—usually about three feet. Closer, if possible. If it is something really rare, shoot a whole role of film at different angles, all close up.

Fig. 7.6. *Turkey poses: A) held by legs with wings and tail spread;*

B) held by head

Fig. 7.7. *Using a timer, this photo could have included the photographer*

Shoot a few specimen shots with a simple background, with and without the hunter in the photo, and be sure to write the critical data about the specimen on the back of the photos, including the date and place taken and the hunter's name and address (Table 7.2).

Even if it is not a freak, you might find that a color closeup of the head makes an interesting picture. If you plan to have the specimen mounted, such a photo may be useful to the taxidermist.

Table 7.2. Information to record about important specimens

Identity of specimen, if necessary (subspecies? sex?)
Weight and other data of interest
Date specimen taken
Who took photos (for credits)
Place (distance and direction to nearest town is good)
Who is in the photos (names)
Name of hunter who took specimen
If for record book, names and addresses of witnesses
Features of interest

Fig. 7.8. *A candid photo taken while the hunter groomed his bird*

Fig. 7.9. Hunter in woods, in hunting clothing, soon after the kill

Photographing Living Turkeys

When on a photographical outing, you can gain access to turkey woods that are off limits to hunting, or you can shoot with the camera when the hunting season is closed. What I most like about photography is that you can shoot the same old gobbler over and over again. When you get the picture you want, it will be a trophy indeed.

Fig. 7.10. This group photo with hens, jakes, and hogs has no outstanding trophies. The trophy is the group photo of family and friends.

Fig. 7.11. *A successful hunter should look pleased, like this lucky Rio hunter from Mississippi. A good photo does not always need the whole turkey or the whole hunter.*

Photographing wildlife is different than photographing your dead turkey, but many of the principles are the same. For wildlife photography, you will need a good camera with a detachable telephoto lens, a tripod, and a blind. You won't need to use a flash, ordinarily. A zoom telephoto lens is ideal but not essential.

Fig. 7.12. *Capture physical features of interest up close. The characteristic reduced white barring is evident in the wing of this Florida gobbler.*

A 35mm single lens reflex camera is the best for all around amateur photography these days. Take a backpack for small items, use an automatic game feeder and other means of baiting, have a folding chair or stool for the blind, and carry most of the same small items you would take when hunting.

Many hunters already have much of the equipment needed. Beware of "expert" advice that emphasizes photography equipment. If you listen to it, you won't have enough money, or time, to take up turkey photography. Expensive equipment makes photography easier, but not any better.

Good wildlife photographs are distinguished by: 1) sharpness of image, which is attained by proper focus and shutter speed; 2) color characteristics, which depend upon the film, its processing, and lighting conditions; 3) the appeal of the subject matter, which depends on your level of patience and creativity; 4) the setting, which depends on how you choose the surroundings to shoot; and 5) composition and postures of the subjects, which mostly depend on good luck when you photograph wild animals.

Most professional outdoor color photography is done with color slide film (also called color reversal film), but if you are doing it for a personal album, you may prefer color print film. Print enlargements suitable for framing can be made from either slides or color negatives.

Fig. 7.13. A good custom-made photo blind

Magazines can use either color negatives or slides, but most prefer slides. If you are serious about taking wild turkey pictures to enlarge and frame, use professional color slide film. Have Illfochrome™ (formerly called "Cibachrome") enlargements made for framing—they resist fading, whereas regular color prints lose their color in time.

Natural lighting in the turkey woods is not good for photography in the morning hours when turkeys usually come to bait sites, and turkeys move around so much it is sometimes difficult to stop them in action with normal film speeds. Use a "fast" film such as ISO 400. You can learn what you need to know about films from a "how-to" photography book if you don't already know enough.

It is not advisable to try to photograph from mere foliage blinds or other natural hiding situations. Use a blind so the turkeys will not see you when you move and make noise.

I have used many types of blinds, including cabana tents, towers, wooden crates, holes in the ground, automobiles, and small structures built on site. My best blind is one designed for turkey field research that utilizes a tractor umbrella and a custom-sewn skirt (Fig. 7.13). Such a blind will cost about $400 if you can find an upholstery shop to make it. Satisfactory ready-made blinds are marketed commercially at prices from about $250 and up—check the ads in hunting magazines and supply catalogs.

The more important features of a good photo blind are: 1) opaque top and sides to darken the interior somewhat so that light will not silhouette your shape and movement inside; 2) waterproof and wind-resistant; 3) roomy enough for two adults plus equipment; and 4) portable.

My blinds have zippered holes in the cloth skirt to permit photographing at different levels and in different directions. The skirts are zippered at two corners to allow the back to be rolled up for ventilation. The bottom edges have small rope loops so they can be staked to the ground in windy situations; guy lines are necessary on especially windy days. My blind can be buttoned up to keep some of the mosquitoes out.

Turkeys and other wild animals become accustomed to blinds of almost any color when they are left in place a few days, but camouflage cloth is a good idea where humans roam unrestrained. The camo effect can be enhanced by adding foliage around the bottom and on top to break the square outlines that turkeys and passing people will recognize as unnatural.

Stationary blinds can be made of tar paper, canvas, plastic sheeting, boards, plywood, or large pieces of corrugated cardboard tacked to trees or posts if you have a place where that is feasible.

Turkeys are easily lured to a photo site with bait. Whole yellow corn is a good bait. Sometimes wheat is good, but it may attract inordinate numbers of blackbirds and other small grain eaters that will not look good in your pictures mixed in with the turkeys.

To attract turkeys to the site, it is a good practice to initially scatter bait in two or three lines radiating out from the photo area for up to one-eighth of a mile. After turkeys take the bait, localize the baiting to a single spot. Be sure there is bait at the site nearly every day.

If turkeys do not come to the site with regularity, you may be too far from their favorite roosting places. Try baiting several spots on the tract and concentrate on the site turkeys seem to use most frequently.

If corn is placed in late afternoon, raccoons and other nocturnal animals will eat it during the night. Better to bait turkeys in the pre-dawn hour. Turkeys usually come to the bait early in the morning and in midafternoon, but if there is bait at the site all day long, they may visit throughout the day.

Using an automatic game feeder will solve most problems associated with baiting irregularity. The type I use is hung from a tree and has a battery-powered clock and timer that dispenses feed automatically at chosen times throughout the day. You can buy a good one for less than $400. Types without timers are less expensive.

Turkeys use bait sites most often during cool weather, but when the fall acorn crop is especially good, they are less interested in grain bait. They are less interested in corn also when the weather is warm. When they are hungry, especially in cool weather, turkeys will remain at a bait site all morning.

Gobblers follow the hens to bait sites in spring and come by to check for hens from time to time. Although adult gobblers do not feed much when hens are present, they will visit bait sites to feed when they do not have strutting in mind.

Some hunters view turkey photography as they do trophy hunting and take their photos under conditions similar to hunting. They like to call their gobblers to the camera. Sometimes you have no other choice. For that style of

Fig. 7.14. *A decoy can be useful in turkey photography to attract turkeys and to stimulate strutting and sometimes fighting*

photography, you need a highly portable blind. I like to use a large piece of camouflaged cloth or netting. I drape it over my head and my small tripod, and cut a hole in it through which to shoot. I roll the cloth up and carry it in a small backpack.

Videography holds great promise for wild turkey enthusiasts. It is easier to take entertaining video footage of moving animals than it is to take good still photos, and it is very easy to show on your home VCR.

If you are doing it only for fun, use the family VHS camcorder. At a more serious level, the new SVHS with three CCD chips and Hi-8 camcorders offer the possibility of broadcast quality images. Equipment costs are near the range of the better home VHS camcorders. The advantage of SVHS and Hi-8 is that copies made from them are very good, whereas copies of VHS usually produce marginal images.

Recording the Turkey's Voice

You can record turkey calls yourself if you really want to understand the turkey's vocabulary and want to have something to review by ear from time to time.

When you make an audio recording, you can take the sounds home and compare the voices of different turkeys and listen for subtleties on the recording you didn't notice in the woods. Even after recording turkeys for more than twenty years, I hear new call variations and gain new insights almost every time I record. When I keep only written notes, it is impossible to compare calls the way I can with my audio collection.

Don't ask electronics experts or recordists for advice on equipment needs unless you have just won the lottery. They chase technology and will insist on exacting specifications you won't understand, can't afford, and don't need. Good recordings are not obtained by electronic sophistication. Excellent recordings are obtained by getting a microphone close to the sound source. Woodscraft, turkey knowledge, common sense, time, patience, and resourcefulness will make up for the shortcomings in electronics. The converse is seldom true.

Recent advances in electronics technology have brought prices of outdoor audio recording equipment into the reach of the average middle class turkey hunter. Basic equipment consists of a small portable audiocassette recorder with noise reduction, an inexpensive tripod, and a directional microphone.

Fig. 7.15. *A parabolic microphone being used to record wild turkeys that were calling on the roost*

Practical audio recorders are available for less than $200 and portable digital audio tape recorders (DATs) are below $600 and getting cheaper every day. Directional microphones are $300 or so and also getting cheaper. A suitable tripod costs only about $40. You can begin recording with less than $1,000 in equipment.

Some of the turkey's calls have never been recorded or named and almost no information is yet available about the turkey's local dialects. Recording turkey calls is an opportunity for the serious naturalist turkey hunter to contribute to a better understanding of the wild turkey. If you have that in mind when you record, be sure to whisper the date, place, and details of the recording on the tape before or after the turkey sounds.

Even if you are not interested in exploring the unknown, recording the turkey's voice will prove to be a fascinating and absorbing off-season way to master the bird's vocabulary. Your turkey hunting friends will enjoy listening to your recordings. Recording and photography go well together to produce unique trophies.

8

How to Dress and Cook a Turkey

A turkey is a trophy to the end. Getting your turkey to the table and enjoying it there is an important part of wild turkey hunting.

Field Dressing

If you plan to eat rather than mount your bird, and cannot completely dress it within two or three hours, it is advisable to remove both the entrails and crop soon after killing it. The entrails will taint the flesh, even in refrigeration, and removing them will aid in cooling the carcass. The crop contains fluids that will sour and give the breast a bad flavor.

If you plan to mount the specimen, forget about eating it and go back to the instructions in Chapter 4.

To remove the entrails, cut a hole in the belly large enough to get your hand in, reach as far toward the neck as you can, and pull everything out. Don't worry about the lungs, liver, and heart. If the liver and heart come out with the other entrails, clean and save them.

The crop is easy to find if it contains food. Feel it from the outside and cut into the skin of the upper breast to get at the thin, elastic crop tissue sac. Separate it from the skin and tear it out. You'll have to cut off the esophagus in the throat where it enters the body cavity.

If the entrails leak some of their contents during the gutting process, rinse the cavity with cool water. Contrary to popular opinion, washing the body cavity will not cause spoilage. Leaving traces of feces in it will.

It goes without saying that a bird keeps better for eating in cold weather than warm. In warm spring weather, the carcass should be refrigerated by midmorning. If it is not immediately refrigerated, at least keep it out of the sun and away from flies. Nothing is gained by aging a dead turkey French-style, but a properly gutted bird will keep unrefrigerated for several hours in cool temperatures.

Preparing the Carcass for Cooking

Turkeys are plucked, skinned, or "breasted-out" for cooking. When a young fall turkey is to be pan fried, skin it whole and cut it up. The skin is not needed for frying.

The breast of an old gobbler is tender enough for frying, but his legs and thighs contain bone slivers and his wings are tough. Use the breast for frying or grilling and use his legs and other parts for soup stock or hash. If the bird is to be smoked, baked, or BBQ'd, pluck it and cook it whole regardless of age. You don't have to eat the tough legs and wings, but they are needed for appearance, if you care about such things.

Skinning

Fried turkey is especially good camp fare because the bird is easy to prepare and to cook with common camp utensils. To skin a turkey for frying, hang the bird by the head and make an incision through the skin around the lower neck. Pull away the skin down the neck and off the breast to the wings and out the wing toward the tip. The skin tears easily. Just keep pulling, cutting, and tearing it off.

Fig. 8.1. *Skinning a turkey for cooking: A) hang the carcass and begin at the neck;*

B) pull and cut skin off down the body;

C) skin the first joint of the wing;

D) cut off the wings (Photos Sandra Prescott)

When the last joint of the wing is reached, cut off and discard the wing tip. If you are to use the wing bones for making yelpers, you may as well cut off the wing where the humerus meets the ulna/radius and remove the bones later.

With the wings skinned or severed, pull the skin downward off the rest of the body. If the specimen is an adult spring gobbler, there will usually be a fatty "breast sponge." The fat is edible but very fattening.

Work the skin down the legs to the joint where the scaly part begins. Cut the skin off the legs at the joint, but leave the lower legs and feet on the carcass to use as handles.

When the base of the tail is reached, cut off the "pope's nose" where the large tail feathers are. The tail and rump feathers can be saved for a wall mount as described in Chapter 4.

Go over the hanging carcass and cut and tear the skin from any remaining areas. Also pick off loose feathers adhering to the carcass. Take any remnants of entrails out of the carcass and wash the bird inside and out.

Breasting out

To breast out a turkey for frying without completely skinning it, make an incision from the crop to the anus, and pull the skin away to expose the breast muscle. Cut the muscle away from the bone in the middle by running the knife next to the bone. Pull and cut the breast muscle away from the bone, one side at a time. After the main muscle is off, cut off any meat pieces you missed. Cut up the breast for frying.

Plucking

The turkey's skin is needed for baking, barbecuing, or smoking. Plucking a turkey is no more trouble than skinning one. A plucked whole turkey is esthetically superior to a skinned one on the dinner platter. Scalding is the best way.

In addition to the things you normally use to prepare any game for the kitchen, you will need the items listed in Table 8.1 for scalding. Cut off the beard before scalding, but leave the legs on for handling the carcass during the scalding and plucking processes. You can remove the spurs after you are through scalding.

Bring to a boil about two gallons of water. Add a tablespoonful of dishwashing detergent. Place the turkey in the tub or cauldron, holding it by the lower legs. With a small pot,

Fig. 8.2. *More skinning: A) skin the rest of the body;*

B) skin the legs;

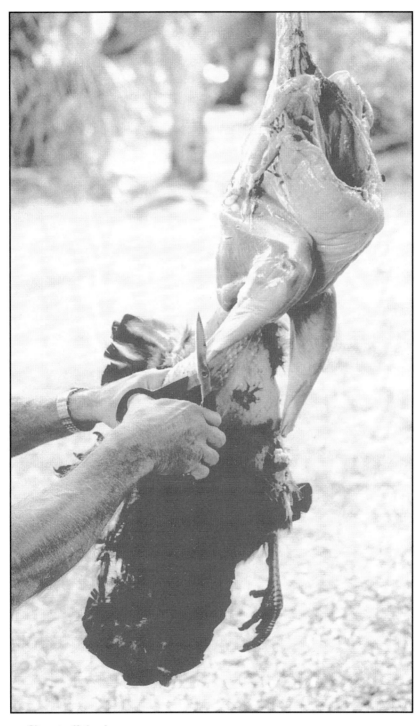

C) cut off the legs;

D) cut off the tail (Photos Sandra Prescott)

dip and pour scalding water over the carcass, being sure to pour water on all the dry places. (You will see the detergent work as the water immediately soaks to the skin.)

Slosh the carcass around in the soapy water to get it soaked, but don't allow any part of the bird to sit in the hot water long enough for the skin to cook. Don't scald the scaly lower legs if you want to save them or the spurs.

When scalding water has been applied to the entire carcass, lay it out and test pluck a few feathers. Test pluck all parts of the plumage so that you can apply more water while it is still hot enough. Use a cup of tap water to dip your fingers in so that you can test pluck without waiting for your fingers to cool in the air.

Pour more scalding water on the base of any feathers that won't pull easily, especially on the wing tips and tail. If you have trouble pulling the large wing feathers, use more scalding water and pliers.

Pull only a few body feathers at a time to prevent the skin from tearing. When you have pulled the feathers that come out easily, pour more scalding water on the rest of the plumage and finish plucking.

If you have not scalded a bird before, on your first one take special care not to overscald the skin, because the skin will tear where it has cooked. You can always use more scalding water if the feathers do not loosen, but you cannot uncook the skin if it becomes overdone.

With practice, you may learn to dip the turkey directly into a tub of hot water and pull it out ready to pluck, but the dip-and-pour method described here is the best way for occasional turkey pluckers.

Table 8.1. Items needed for scalding a wild turkey

Item	Purpose
Tub or cauldron	Hold the hot water
Long-handled pot or dipper	Dip and pour scalding water
Tablespoon of dish detergent	Wetting agent
Fire or substitute	Produce scalding water
Cup of cool water	Cool your fingers as you pluck
Newspaper	Lay bird and wet feathers on
Clean pan	Hold plucked bird to finish job
Small container	Hold liver, heart, and gizzard

You can "dry" pluck a turkey without scalding, but the process is more difficult and gets feathers all over the place. Do it while the carcass is still warm and limber, in the woods, right after shooting it.

You will find it difficult to pull out the large wing and tail feathers without scalding, even if the carcass is still warm, and when you get back to camp with a dry-picked turkey, you won't have much to show or photograph.

After the bird is plucked, remove the lower legs and head, leaving only a two-inch length of neck on the carcass—a longer neck will get in the way during cooking.

Some people cut off the last joint of the wing instead of pulling the large feathers. Either way is okay, but a baked turkey looks better on the table with its wings on. A couple of cups of properly placed scalding water will loosen the toughest wing feathers. Cooked wing bones are okay for making yelpers, so don't worry about that.

Do not remove the fatty tissue under the breast skin of an adult spring gobbler if it is to be plucked and cooked whole— the fat makes your gobbler a naturally basted bird as seen on TV and in the grocery store.

If you saved the liver, heart, and gizzard, open the gizzard, remove the contents, and pull off the inside lining. Find the small greenish gall bladder in the liver and remove it with a sharp knife, then rinse the liver. The heart requires no special treatment.

Cooking

Cooking directions for domestic turkeys apply to wild turkeys. I'll mention only the traditional cooking methods. If you want more, look in a good cookbook such as the *L. L. Bean Game & Fish Cookbook* or any standard cookbook.

Cooking a whole turkey

Table 8.2. Oven baking time for whole turkeys in 325°F oven

Weight of dressed bird (pounds)	Time, unstuffed (hours)	Time, stuffed[a] (hours)
8	2-1/2	2-3/4
10	2-3/4	3
12	3	3-1/2
14	3-1/2	4

[a] Assumes the stuffing is precooked.

If you plan to stuff the turkey, precook the stuffing. There is no way to cook anything inside the bird's carcass without overcooking the outside of it. You will find other advantages to cooking and serving the dressing separately. It won't hurt to stick an onion or apple in the body cavity as a source of moisture during cooking, but you don't need to.

Tie the legs across the open body cavity and pull them together to close the cavity. Tie the wings to each other with twine across the breast. Rub the skin with whatever you like— pepper, salt, oil, butter, garlic, or vinegar, but do not add BBQ sauce at this stage—it will begin to char before the bird is cooked. If the bird is to be charcoal baked and BBQ sauce is desired, apply it as you finish cooking or serve it as a side dish.

The traditional ways to cook a whole turkey are oven baking, plain smoking, smoke-cooking, and charcoal roasting. The differences are what you cook in, the level of heat, the amount of smoke, and the total time in the smoker/cooker.

Oven baking takes 2-1/2 to 4 hours depending on the temperature, the size of the bird, and whether or not the bird is stuffed. Plain smoking a gobbler takes 10-12 hours; smoke-cooking 6-8 hours; roasting over coals 3-4 hours. Table 8.3 shows the major differences among the ways to cook a whole turkey.

Oven baking. You can use any baking procedure recommended for a domestic turkey, including stuffing and covering with a baking bag or roaster lid. Some recipes call for changing oven temperature and covering and uncovering the bird during the cooking process. All those methods work. I prefer to cook the turkey covered then remove the cover for final browning.

If you follow the cookbook for domestic turkeys, reduce the recommended cooking time by about fifteen to twenty percent. The thin body structure of a wild turkey does not require as much baking as does a rotund domestic turkey.

Table 8.3. Approximate cooking time for whole turkeys by different methods

Method	Temperature	Time
Oven roasting	325°F	15 min./lb.
Full smoking	Warm smoke only	10 hours
Smoke cooking	Coals and smoke source	6-8 hours
Frying	Very hot—400°F	2 minutes per side[a]

[a] Breast should be fried only briefly to golden color, not browned.

An overcooked wild turkey tastes like an overcooked domestic one—dry. Be sure the cook knows there is nothing about a wild turkey that calls for sentencing to long confinement in the oven.

Concern for parasites in wild game is unfounded. Humans have not been in the Western Hemisphere long enough for wild animal parasites to evolve ways to invade us. The life cycles of parasites require specific intermediate hosts and complex life cycles. There is nothing in a fresh wild turkey that you can catch, even if you eat it raw. So it is not necessary to parboil, salt soak, marinate, tenderize, radiate, or sanitize a wild turkey for human consumption. Neither do you need to stuff fruits, vegetables, other animals, other parts of animals, or other things inside the body cavity. Do nothing to a wild turkey you would not do to a domestic one, except don't roast it quite as long.

Smoking. Many local welders make good smokers that can be used for plain smoking, smoke-cooking, or charcoal roasting. My favorite smoker was made in Old Town, Florida from bottled gas cylinders (Fig. 8.3). It has a separate compartment for making wood smoke and is adaptable to almost any mode of cooking.

Fig. 8.3. A domestic turkey and a wild turkey early in the smoking process. When fully smoked, the blackened skin will be removed and not eaten.

Plain smoking is best done without heating the turkey above about 120°F. Since the temperature is not very hot, you do not have to closely tend the smoking process—just keep the smoke rolling. A smoked turkey's skin, which will be almost black, should be removed before eating. Smoking does not work with a skinned turkey.

Smoke-cooking. My favorite way to cook a whole turkey is over a charcoal fire in a smoker that can be closed for partial smoking.

Most so-called smokers are actually smoke-cookers. For smoke-cooking, use heat under the bird and plenty of smoke. The popular dome-shaped manufactured "smokers" with moisture pans work well for smoke-cooking and require little attention.

Charcoal roasting. For charcoal roasting, use more heat and less smoke than for smoke-cooking. Cooking time over charcoal depends on the size of the bird and level of heat, and requires a little more attention than other methods because of the possibility of burning. Keep the charcoal fire short of flaming up, with the bird about ten to twelve inches from the coals. If too much fat is dripping into the fire, raise the bird or dampen the heat.

It is a good practice to push the hot coals out from directly under the turkey—make an open circle so that the fat will drip in the open spot and not on hot coals. The turkey will cook more evenly that way, with less attention, and the fire will not flame up.

Keep the turkey's back to the fire for most of the cooking process to prevent the breast from overcooking. Check the bird frequently to avoid charring. Turn it as the skin browns. The less experience you have in BBQing turkeys, the more you need to check it.

When using a rotisserie, balance the bird on the spit before placing it on the fire. Follow the procedures recommended for your equipment.

Whole hickory nuts dropped a few at a time into the coals make an ideal smoke source. The nuts can be used green directly from the tree, husks and all. They are convenient to store and have a high concentration of the substances that make hickory wood a good smoking wood. If dried nuts are used, soak them a few hours in water.

Red bay is a good smoking wood, as are oak, mesquite, and buttonwood. Everywhere smoking is done, there is a favorite smoking wood—use whatever is in vogue in your neighborhood, but do not use soft woods such as pine, fir, cedar, or spruce. (If you didn't already know that, put the turkey back on ice while you read a BBQ book.)

Spring gobblers and adult fall hens usually have enough natural fat to keep the breast well basted while they smoke or roast. I usually baste juvenal turkeys lightly a couple of times with vegetable oil and sometimes squeeze a fresh grapefruit or orange on the cooking bird.

The giblets will fry up with the rest of the bird, if the bird is fried, or can be chopped and used in gravy with baked turkey or to go with rice or another starchy dish. If gravy is to be made, you may as well save the neck and boil it to make gravy stock.

If you saved the legs and thighs of an old gobbler, boil them until the meat falls off the bones, remove the main bones and the splinter bones, and use the meat and stock for soup and gravy.

You can roast a turkey in the kitchen oven until it is about half done and finish it in a smoker to pick up the smoked flavor; or you can reverse the process and start it in the smoker and finish it in the oven.

Carving a whole turkey

Carve a wild turkey as you would a tame one, with a sharp carving knife, large fork, and large platter. You may need a second platter for the carved meat and tongs for serving. You will need to touch the bird with your fingers as you carve; you can do it bare-handed or use a cloth cooking glove on one hand. If you do it bare-handed, wash your hands in front of all the guests before you start.

Slide the turkey carefully from the cooker to the platter to keep the carcass intact. With the fork, push one of the legs to the side. It will usually separate at the joint between the thigh and body or at the drumbone. If it doesn't separate, cut the whole leg off at the junction of the thigh and body.

If the drumbone pulls out of the leg in your hand, it means you have slightly overcooked the bird. Put the bone where it won't be thrown out after dinner and use it in making a yelper. If the bone doesn't pull out of the leg, hold the small end of the drumstick with the fingers and, with the knife, separate it from the thigh. Continue to hold the drumstick and slice the meat off it parallel to the bone onto the plate. If it is an old turkey, the

Fig. 8.4. Wild and domestic turkey on the platter. Which is which?

drumstick tendons will have ossified into "splinter bones." Lay the drumstick aside and plan to pick out the splinter bones when you make soup. The thigh of an old gobbler will be a little tough but edible—remove and slice it parallel to the bone. Save the femur bone for making yelpers. Put the bone up as soon as you finish carving so your aunt will not throw it out when she helps with the cleanup.

Next, tackle the wing on the same side you are working on by pushing it away from the body with the fork. Cut it off where it joins the body. (The joint is probably deeper in the shoulder of the breast than you thought.) Lay aside the wing to serve whole or cut it up. Don't forget to salvage the wing bones immediately after dinner.

With the wing and leg removed, one side of the breast will be exposed. Slice the breast thinly, parallel to the body, using short strokes. The slices will fall away from the body and pile up on each other.

If one side of the bird furnishes enough meat to begin dinner, leave the other half for later carving—it will remain warmer and moister if left uncarved. When you need more turkey, do the same to the other side of the bird.

After taking the legs, wings, and major breast meat, there is still more turkey there, but the process of getting it is less artistic. That is a good time to tell a story about the hunt to divert attention from the carving.

The bony carcass should be saved and the meat boiled off the bones to make soup. Boil it the same day and save the soup ingredients in the refrigerator. If you plan to use cooked turkey bones to make yelpers, do not permit them to be boiled for long periods in making stock or soup. Excessive boiling will cause bone softening. Take them out before putting the scraps in the soup pot.

Grilled turkey breast

Grilling over charcoal is one way to cook the breast you have salvaged from a specimen destined for the taxidermist or taken from a gobbler with legs and wings too tough to cook.

Use any seasoning you like—black pepper and garlic powder are usually enough. Hold the salt until you are ready to eat it. Get the coals very hot and grill the breast in large pieces, close to the coals, as you would small beef steaks. Do not cook it any longer than you would a rare beef steak. Do not brown it. Turkey breast gets tougher the longer you cook it.

Fried turkey

Wild turkey has traditionally been fried by hunters and housewives. Edward A. McIlhenny recommended frying wild turkey in his wild turkey book written in 1914. Breast meat of even old gobblers is tender. Fried turkey breast "fingers" came long before anybody ever heard of chicken "nuggets" or "tenders."

A turkey to be fried is normally skinned. If you cut up a turkey as you would a chicken for frying, the pieces will be too large. It is best to bone out a turkey and cut up the large pieces.

Cut up a skinned or plucked young turkey by removing the scaly lower legs and most of the neck. Remove the wings and cut them into frying-sized pieces. Bone out most of the thigh into about eight to ten pieces. The breast should be removed, one slab from each side, and sliced into frying-sized pieces—each piece about the size of two fingers.

The drumstick of even a young fall turkey contains a few ossified tendons that need to be removed for frying. Cut the raw meat from the drumstick in four or five pieces parallel to the bone and remove each tendon with a knife. (If it's an old turkey, lay the drumstick aside along with the wings to use them for soup stock.)

Dip the pieces in buttermilk and shake them in a double grocery paper bag containing flour or cracker meal, or use any method of battering you would for frying chicken or fish.

Fry in about one inch of cooking oil in a covered cast iron skillet or chicken fryer over medium-high heat. Turn each piece to lightly brown both sides and finish the pieces with the top off the fryer.

Most cooks overcook the white breast meat of birds such as chicken, quail, turkey, and grouse. The best procedure is to remove the breast pieces from the skillet *just before* they are brown—a very light golden color is just right. Try undercooking white breast meat and you will probably have discovered how to cook it to perfection.

You can fry a turkey whole if you have a cauldron or some other very large pot, a hot fire source such as a fish cooker, and several gallons of cooking oil. Salt and pepper the whole plucked or skinned bird and drop it into deep frying fat. Fry it for approximately half an hour. Let it cool for a few minutes and cut it up for serving.

However you plan to cook your turkey, don't let it work its way to the bottom of the deep freezer. Eat it on the very next suitable occasion. A deceased wild turkey deserves at least that much respect.

For Turkey Hunting Information	Subspecies Present	Native
Georgia Department of Natural Resources 2070 U. S. Hwy. 278 SE Social Circle, GA 30279	Eastern	Eastern
Hawaii Division of Forestry & Wildlife 1151 Punchbowl St. Honolulu, HI 96813	Rio Grande Feral	None
Ildaho Game & Fish Box 25 Boise, ID 83707	Merriam's Rio Grande	None
Illinois Department of Conservation Rt. 2, Box 628 Jonesboro, IL 62952	Eastern	Eastern
Indiana Division of Fish & Wildlife 402 W. Washington St., Rm. W273 Indianapolis, IN 46205	Eastern	Eastern
Iowa Department of Natural Resources Wallace State Office Bldg. Des Moines, IA 50319	Eastern	Eastern
Kansas Department of Wildlife & Parks 512 SE 25th Ave. Pratt, KS 67124	Eastern Rio Grande Hybrid	Eastern
Kentucky Department of Fish, Wildlife & Parks #1 Game Farm Rd. Frankfort, KY 40601	Eastern	Eastern
Louisiana Department of Wildlife & Fisheries Box 278 Tioga, LA 71360	Eastern	Eastern
Maine Department of Inland Fisheries & Wildlife 284 State St. Augusta, ME 04333	Eastern	Eastern
Maryland Wildlife Division Tri-State Office Bldg. Annapolis, MD 20401	Eastern	Eastern

For Turkey Hunting Information	Subspecies Present	Native
Massachusetts Division of Fisheries & Wildlife 1 Rabbit Hill Rd. Westborough, MA 01581	Eastern	Eastern
Michigan Department of Natural Resources Box 30028 Lansing, MI 48909	Eastern	Eastern
Minnesota Department of Natural Resources 500 Lafayette Rd. St. Paul, MN 55155-4007	Eastern	Eastern
Mississippi Department of Wildlife Box 451 Jackson, MS 39205	Eastern	Eastern
Missouri Department of Conservation Box 180 Jefferson City, MO 65102-0180	Eastern	Eastern
Montana Department of Fish, Wildlife & Parks 1420 E. 6th Ave. Helena, MT 59620	Merriam's	None
Nebraska Game & Parks Box 30370 Lincoln, NE 68503	Merriam's Hybrid	Eastern
New Hampshire Fish & Game Department 2 Hazen Dr. Concord, NH 03301	Eastern	Eastern
New Jersey Division of Game, Fish & Wildlife CN400 Trenton, NJ 08625	Eastern	Eastern
New Mexico Department of Game & Fish Box 25112 Santa Fe, NM 87504	Merriam's	Merriam's
New York Bureau of Wildlife, Game Bird Unit Wildlife Resources Ctr. Delmar, NY 12054	Eastern	Eastern

For Turkey Hunting Information	Subspecies Present	Native
North Carolina Wildlife Resources Commission 512 N. Salisbury St. Raleigh, NC 27604-1118	Eastern	Eastern
North Dakota State Game & Fish Department Box 7 Oakes, ND 58474	Eastern Merriam's Hybrid	None
Ohio Division of Wildlife 1840 Belcher Dr. Columbus, OH 43224	Eastern	Eastern
Oklahoma Department of Fish & Wildlife Box 53465 Oklahoma City, OK 73152	Eastern Rio Grande Hybrid	Eastern Rio Grande
Oregon Department of Fish & Wildlife Box 59 Portland, OR 97207	Merriam's Rio Grande Hybrid	None
Pennsylvania Game Commission 2001 Elmerton Ave. Harrisburg, PA 17110-9797	Eastern	Eastern
Rhode Island Division of Fish & Wildlife 4808 Tower Hill Rd. Wakefield, RI 02679	Eastern	Eastern
South Carolina Wildlife & Marine Resources Department Drawer 190 Bonneau, SC 29431	Eastern	Eastern
Tennessee Wildlife Resources Agency Box 4047 Nashville, TN 37204	Eastern	Eastern
Texas Parks & Wildlife Department 4200 Smith School Rd. Austin, TX 78744	Eastern Rio Grande	Rio Grande*

* Turkey populations native to east Texas, extirpated but later restored, may have been the Eastern subspecies.

For Turkey Hunting Information	Subspecies Present	Native
Utah Division of Wildlife Resources 1596 W. North Temple Salt Lake City, UT 84116	Merriam's Rio Grande	None
Vermont Fish & Wildlife Department 103 S. Main St. Waterbury, VT 05671-0501	Eastern	Eastern
Virginia Department of Game & Inland Fisheries Box 996 Verona, VA 24482	Eastern	Eastern
Washington Department of Wildlife 600 N. Capitol Way Olympia, WA 98501-1091	Merriam's Rio Grande	None
West Virginia Wildlife Resources Division State Capitol Complex, Bldg. 3 Charleston, WV 25305	Eastern	Eastern
Wisconsin Department of Natural Resources Box 7921 Madison, WI 53707	Eastern	Eastern
Wyoming Game & Fish Department 5400 Bishop Blvd. Cheyenne, WY 82006	Merriam's	None

Literature Cited

Bland, Dwain. 1986. *The turkey hunter's digest.* DBI Books, Northbrook, Illinois.

Cameron, Angus and Judith Jones. 1983. *The L. L. Bean game & fish cookbook.* Random House, New York, New York.

Harbour, Dave. 1983. *Advanced wild turkey hunting & world records.* Winchester Press, Piscataway, New Jersey.

Harlan, Howard L. 1994. *Turkey calls.* Harland/Anderson Press [Location not given].

Kennamer, James E. and Mary C. Kennamer. 1990. Current status and distribution of the wild turkey. Pages 1-12 *in* Healy, W. M. and G. B. Healy, Editors, *Sixth National Wild Turkey Symposium* 1-12.

Langston, Jay. 1995. New Rio Grande record surfaces, tops wild turkey records. *The Caller* 6: 54-61.

McDowell, R. D. 1956. Productivity of the wild turkey in Virginia. Ph. D. Thesis. Virginia Polytechnic Institute, Blacksburg, Virginia.

McKusick, Charmion R. 1980. Three groups of turkeys from southwestern archaeological sites. *Contri. Sci. Natur. Hist. Mus. Los Angeles County* 330:225-235.

Mickel, Earl. 1994. *Turkey callmakers past and present.* Published by the author. 253 pp.

Rea, Amadeo M. 1980. Late Pleistocene and Holocene turkeys in the southwest. *Contri. Sci. Natur. Hist. Mus. Los Angeles County* 330:209-224.

Schorger, A. W. 1957. The beard of the wild turkey. *Auk* 74:441-446.

————. 1966. *The wild turkey: its history and domestication.* University of Oklahoma Press, Norman, Oklahoma.

Stangel, Peter W., Paul L. Leberg, and Julia I. Smith. 1994. Systematics and population genetics. Pages 18-28 *in* Dickson, James G., Editor, *The wild turkey: biology and management.* Stackpole, Harrisburg, Pennsylvania.

Steadman, David W. 1980. A review of the osteology and paleontology of turkeys (Aves: Meleagaridinae). *Contrib. Sci. Natur. Hist. Mus. Los Angeles County* 330:131-207.

Wetmore, Alexander. 1931. The avifauna of the Pleistocene in Florida. *Smithsonian Misc. Colls.* 82:33-35.

Williams, Lovett E., Jr. 1961. Notes on wing molt in the yearling wild turkey. *J. Wildl. Manage.* 25:439-440.

———. 1981. *The book of the wild turkey.* Winchester Press, Tulsa, Oklahoma.

———. 1984. *The voice and vocabulary of the wild turkey.* Real Turkeys Publishers, Gainesville, Florida.

———. *The art & science of wild turkey hunting.* Real Turkeys Publishers, Gainesville, Florida.

Williams, Lovett E., Jr. and D. H. Austin. 1988. *Studies of the wild turkey in Florida.* University Presses of Florida, Gainesville, Florida.

Williams, Lovett E., Jr. and R. D. McGuire. 1971. On prenuptial molt in the wild turkey. *J. Wildl. Manage.* 35: 394-395.

Wunz, Gerald A. 1992. Wild turkeys outside their historic range. Pages 361-384 *in* Dickson, James G., Editor, *The wild turkey: biology and management.* Stackpole, Harrisburg, Pennsylvania.

Index